Grea in

W

Plains Publishing Inc.
Edmonton

Canadian Cataloguing in Publication Data

O'Callaghan, William John, 1937 -
  Great balls of fire.

  ISBN 0-920985-36-X

  I. Title.

PS8579.C34G7 1987   C813'.54   C87-091504-5
PR9199.3.033G7 1987

Cover by Gundra Kucy
Edited by Alice Major

Plains Publishing Inc.
10316 - 121 Street
Edmonton, Alberta
T5N 1K8

The publishers gratefully acknowledge the support of the Alberta Foundation for the Literary Arts.

Printed and Bound in Canada.

Contents

Dedication

To Steve Woodman

1 MUSIC! MUSIC! MUSIC!

The sex lecture in high school had ended before the relationship between bees and flowers was discussed. Our class felt deprived of vital information. To fill the gap, I sat on the back steps at home and scrutinized a bumblebee humming among pink and white blossoms. When the sweet-peas were picked clean, the insect hovered in a lazy circle and, sensing the evening air, aimed its flight at me. A flash of auburn and snap of closing jaws sent the bee in a swift arc upward.

"Good pup," I said to Clancy, who shook his reddish-brown cocker spaniel ears and settled in a new position watching the crab-apple tree where the bee had disappeared. "T.J. doesn't approve of '*eau de lettoochie*' but at least something's attracted to it." Clancy snorted but kept his distance.

Thomas Joseph Reilly, my stepfather, had given an ultimatum: either bathe and change clothes after returning from Safeway's produce department or take my lettuce-cabbage-turnip presence outside and eat supper on the porch. This warm Saturday, August 27, 1955, outdoors was more appealing than the humid kitchen. I followed Clancy's gaze.

"Come on, pup. Let's check the crop."

Using our fence as a vault, I sprang and boosted past the garage eave onto the roof. The old, black shingles were loose and required a square-footed walk over the apex to the opposite side. I eased nearer the laden branches. The sweet apples were ripe. Balancing on one foot and grasping a drooped branch, I plucked the largest apple from a cluster. Clancy was waiting below, tail wagging, mouth agape and tongue poised. I polished the fruit with my palms, twisted out the stem and dropped the morsel through a gap in the leaves; Clancy caught it and trotted back to his doghouse. He never ate apples off the ground but would secure a hand-picked one between his paws and nibble it to the core.

I turned toward the other tree. The red, sour crab-apples were bunched like cherries. A movement caught my eye. Beyond the peak of the roof, a familiar head with prematurely grey hair was passing on the nearby avenue.

"Impossible," I thought. "He never comes here." Easing up, I looked again. There was no mistake. I sat, hoping the figure would continue eastbound. "I don't," I muttered, "need a pep talk. Not now. Not tonight."

Clancy's ears perked. The iron front gate creaked open and clicked shut. The wind? Too calm. The doorbell buzzed. The paperboy? He collected last night. Mother's voice came through the back door screen window; she spoke in a tone used only for greeting visiting clergy.

"Why Father Fee, what a surprise! Do come in."

Make an escape? He might linger all night. Flatten on the garage roof?

The dog would look at me and yap his fool head off to announce a stranger in the yard. Would the priest come to the back? No doubt about it.

"There's someone here to see you," Mother sang. T.J. was at his club. My younger brother Mickey had wolfed his supper and gone to a movie. I was the only you around.

"Be right there, Mom," I called, taking a short-cut through the tree to the lawn.

Father Fee descended the steps as I approached. There was a momentary silence.

"May we talk?" he asked, motioning toward the stairs. He sat on the middle step without first brushing away the dirt. Father Fee was a perfect gentleman and tried to put everyone in his presence at ease. By not cleaning the board's surface he assumed our house, inside and out, had been swept moments before his unscheduled arrival. The dust would show on his black suit unless he had plans to stay until nightfall. I glanced at the sky. The sun was starting to set. There would be at least an hour of twilight. He *did* want to talk.

"Sit please," he said.

Clancy, who had been snuffling around the black shoes, obediently sat down. I settled on the cement walk and rested my back on the doghouse. From six feet away, I was reassured by Father Fee's clerical smell of starch. The breeze was in the right direction. He would not be able to detect my lettuce odor.

"Still working at Safeway?"

"Yes, Father, but only on Saturdays. During the week I'm at the Imperial Oil refinery."

"Doing what?"

"Yard Crew. We're with the painters, carpenters, boilermakers, ditch diggers, gardeners, warehouse, railroaders and everything."

"Why do you hold down two jobs? Surely one would be enough to pay your university expenses."

"Yes, Father." I knew what was next.

"You *are* going to university this fall?"

"Yes, Father, but I need," I said, trying to change the subject, "a job during the school year to pay for books and stuff."

"Stuff? Like dates?" A smile flickered across his face as he caught his own pun.

"Yeah," I took the cue, "dates and gas for the car and beer and all that."

"Beer? Indeed! I'd understood you'd given up on engineering. Dentistry, isn't it?"

"I'm not sure, Father," I replied. "In Grade Ten it was engineering; in Grade Eleven it was orthodontics and now I don't know."

Father Fee was suddenly interested. "Tell me about it."

"When I had braces on my teeth I figured by the time dentistry and the post-grad orthodontics program were over Dr. Quigley would be ready to retire. He's the only orthodontist in Edmonton."

"And so?"

"And so I talked with our family dentist and he said to go as far as I could with my education and get a job where I wouldn't be on my feet all day."

"And you chose...?"

"... a combined pre-med and pre-dent program for the first year. I can be either a doctor or a dentist."

The priest's shoulders slumped. As the shadows began to fall, his face darkened. He thought a long while, as if struggling to find precisely the correct way of broaching a distasteful subject. I shifted on the pavement.

"What," he asked finally, "is it?"

"What's what, Father?"

"What is wrong with you guys?"

"Pardon?"

"One vocation. From the entire graduating class of St. Joseph's High School, we are getting exactly one seminarian. I've just come from his home."

My mind raced through the possibilities. Red and Mert lived further east; Father Fee had been walking east when I first spied him so it wasn't either of them. Robert and Richard had always lived west but there was no way Richard would enter the priesthood. Ape's family had recently moved west.

"Robert?" I asked.

"No, it's Peter."

"Ape?" I could believe it. "Are you sure, Father?"

"Peter seems to be, but whether it is God's will or not, no one knows. May I ask you once more? What's wrong with you grads?"

"Maybe it was a bad year."

Father Fee's face began to swell. There was an impression of a volcano about to erupt. "Bad year?" he said, raising his voice. The words began to spew out like molten lava. "A bad three years with your whole group. You decimated our once-proud teaching staff. Let me list off your class triumphs, if I may call them that. There was poor old Father Daly, twenty-four years as St. Joe's principal, finished after Grade Ten."

My older step-brother, Pat, warned me about Father Daly, saying that he was sly, vengeful and would cut anyone off at the knees without a moment's hesitation. My sole confrontation with him had been in the Grade Ten math class. Father Daly, during one of his droning discourses, had told a joke. "Where," he asked, "does a cowboy keep his wife?" When no one replied, he gave the answer: "Home on the range, of course." There was mandatory laughter from the class but Father Daly's piercing frown brought silence. "Don't you get it?" he asked, looking at me. "You're not laughing." I replied that I got the joke but did not think it was funny. Muffled gasps filled the room. I was about to die. "Well," said the priest, looking at the yellowed page, "scratch one bad joke." One deleted groaner did not end a career. The incident with Red must have been the final straw.

Red, a full-blooded Blackfoot Indian, was an original member of our St. John's Elementary School gang. In Grade Seven, he had conducted basement experiments in chemistry, one of which had exploded and imbedded a metallic fragment above his right eyebrow, giving him a permanent quizzical expression. In Grade Eight, he was drawing various atoms, complete with proton-neutron nuclei and their correct complement of electron rings, on the school blackboard. In Grade Nine, he received a patent from Ottawa for his version of a perpetual motion machine. In Grade Ten, accustomed to direct, no-nonsense thinking, he was becoming agitated in our math class. Father Daly had spent the entire month of September discussing the reasoning behind a mathematical point—represented by a chalk dot on the board. In October, we endured the addition of a second dot while in November, a line appeared between the two spots. December was marked by the conclusion that the shortest distance between the two points was a straight line.

Father Daly was bursting with enthusiasm over this revelation. "In over a quarter century of teaching, not one student has disagreed with this fact. Is there anyone here who does?"

I glanced at Red. His head was down—a sign something was about to happen. Red's hawk-like nose and sweeping black eyes reminded me of an eagle about to pounce on its prey. Still facing the desk top, he raised his right hand: he was preparing to dive.

"Mr. Redfeather seems to disagree," said the startled teacher. "Will you favor us with your words of wisdom, Gordon?"

"Suppose," said Red looking at Father Daly, "both points are moving."

"We are talking," replied Father in a paternal, patient reiteration, "about mathematical theory. You understand? Theory."

"Then," Red smiled, "in theory there is no such thing as a straight line between A and B. To draw it, you have to go half way, then half of the remainder and half again of what's left forever. In theory you can never get from A to B."

The bell rang. The period ended. Father Daly was left staring at the diagram and moving his lips; he might have been saying a prayer of last rites over his lecture notes.

I eased my back off the doghouse.

"But Father, we dedicated the 1954 Year Book to him."

"Some consolation," Father Fee continued. "The teacher every other class called 'Easy Ed'. You gave the poor man ulcers."

I could not recall a specific incident. There were three rooms of Grade Twelve boys. One of the other groups must have got him. I passed on that one.

"And Father Kelly. High blood pressure. The doctors ordered him to a country parish for some rest. That incident, by the way, almost had you expelled."

"Me?"

"Yes, you. Frank Schneider saved your hide. He told us centuries of theologians hadn't answered your question and you could hardly be faulted for asking. But why did you bring it up at all?"

The episode occurred in religion class. Father Kelly was discussing the biblical passage about Jesus' brothers and sisters who were outside waiting to visit.

"The reference, of course, was from a translation. The original word for close relatives could mean brothers, sisters, cousins and the like. This mention obviously meant cousins."

I raised my hand and, at the priest's nod, said, "Does it really matter?"

"Explain yourself, please."

"Whether or not Jesus had brothers and sisters, His teachings remain the same."

Father Kelly was irritated. "Of course it matters. We are speaking here of Our Blessed Virgin. Do you understand? Virgin."

"Sure, before Jesus was born, but does it matter what happened after?"

The teacher's hands were closing into fists. "Are you suggesting Our Lady had carnal knowledge?"

"She was married, wasn't she?"

"Yes." The priest spat the word through clenched teeth.

"And carnal knowledge in marriage isn't wrong so she could have had other kids and still stayed free of sin."

"I said virgin, you ignoramus."

That did it. Father Kelly wanted to play hardball. Up until this remark the question game had been between pitcher and catcher; he had now entered the batter's box and struck a foul blow. I decided to bean him.

"Does that mean Jesus was born by Caesarian section?" I asked in an innocent voice.

Father's face turned purple. The large vein on his forehead stood out. The beanball had hit home. He sputtered, "Are you suggesting the birth of Our Lord broke the..." He could not bring himself to say more. "That's utter blasphemy." He was now screaming. "Blasphemy! Get out of here. This instant."

The exchange was not mentioned again until that August evening. Mother had turned on the porch light. Clancy chased a moth. Father Fee continued his roll call.

"Mr. McEleney's hands were trembling so badly, after that typing class, he couldn't hold a cup of coffee."

"I took shorthand, Father."

"Yes, but you must know the scuttlebutt. He was conducting a speed test in typing. When he said, 'Go', every key tapped in slow unison and every typewriter bell in the class plinked at the same time. He stopped the test and ordered the papers turned in. Every one of them was complete and letter-perfect. How did they do it?"

"Everyone typed the lesson the day before."

"Then why weren't there extra letters on the papers, or misalignments?"

"They used the capitalize buttons and..."

"... and the space bar," Father Fee sighed. "Speaking about doubting one's sanity, I've seen requests for transfer at the end of a year but when your physics teacher was in the office blubbering after one period, that had to be a record."

I recalled the caper. Richard found a live mouse in his locker on the first school day after summer vacation; he brought it to the classroom and secured a saddle on the rodent. We sat quietly. The physics teacher strode in. Hands on hips and feet apart, he faced us and snarled, "I hear you think you're tough. I'll show you this year what tough *really* is! I'm a former pro hockey player and I earned the nickname Tiger for good reason. I eat up anybody that crosses me. Got it?" He turned to the blackboard and scribbled several lines. "This is the text you need. Got it?" Tiger's hand reached for the eraser; he was going to rub out the book name as quickly as it was written. The eraser had moved to the far end of the rail. Tiger showed his toughness by obliterating the chalk with his sleeve. He walked to the other side. "For those of you over here wearing glasses, these are the supplies you need." He wrote on the board, turned briefly toward our cherubic faces and said again, "Got it?" Tiger kept his eyes on us while groping for the eraser; it was now at the central part of the rail. "So," he sneered, pointing to the neat knot on the eraser's upper surface, "you thought you'd fool me with the old hidden string trick did you? Okay, you miserable wretches," he said, grabbing the eraser and holding it aloft, "let's see if any of you punks can yank this out of my hand. No? I thought as much." Tiger smiled triumphantly, slammed the brush on the board and smeared blood, guts and mouse fur over the green surface. He stared. He retched. He exited stage left.

Father Fee shifted to the next step up and extended his legs. "Need I go on?" he asked. "The list is almost endless. There was the substitute teacher episode and the sex lecture fiasco. But of all the things I never expected, there was Father Mac. A tower of strength broken. I can't pin it down but I'm sure you people had a hand in it."

"But Father, we dedicated the 1955 Year Book to him."

"How generous. Now we surviving teachers have to endure the ultimate insult. Did I say decimated our ranks? Devastated would be more apt. Do you know the end result of your three years of organized mayhem at St. Joseph's?"

"No, Father."

"Awards Night. First time we've had one. The School Board has told us to organize a gala evening to reward the bunch of you."

I was amazed. "How come?"

"Evidently," the priest continued, "in concert with that chaos and destruction, your class also totally conquered the Grade Twelve Departmental Examinations. Honor marks in every subject; scholarships galore; the best St. Joe's record in living memory. City championship in football. First-ever chess championship. I can't understand it. What's going on? Why did Mr. Schneider emerge unscathed? You guys think he's great. Why have you allowed me to retain my senses? My classes were models of decorum. What is happening with you fellows? Look, I've known your family since you were a toddler on 115th Street. Give me a straight answer."

"I dunno, Father."

"Thanks a lot."

"Maybe it was the girls."

"I thought of that but they're not to blame. Their arrival at St. Joe's had to be a coincidence. The same change is going on in Calgary and boys' and girls' schools are not amalgamated yet."

"Just Calgary?"

"No, all over. Sweeping changes. The Catholic schools seem to be hit first and hit hardest in any given area but it's happening everywhere. The Archbishop has contacts throughout North America; he saw it coming two years ago. Subtle changes then; unmistakable now. That about coincides with your time in high school. Any clues? Any idea why you and your compatriot teenagers have linked together to form something like a giant living organism with totally different standards?"

"Maybe we're glad to be alive."

Father Fee looked upward. "My God in heaven, is that the answer?" He waited. "No reply. Try again."

"Sorry, Father, I can't think of anything else."

The priest bent forward, elbows on his knees, as if confiding a secret password. "The Archbishop," he said quietly, "is convinced the root of all the trouble is rock and roll music."

I burst out laughing. "You've got to be kidding. Like what?"

"*Rock Around the Clock*, for instance."

I could barely contain myself. "That's new, Father. It hasn't been around for two or three years."

"All right, how about *Shake, Rattle And Roll*."

"Still new. What else you got?"

"*Roll With Me Henry*."

"That's *Dance With Me Henry*, Father." I was stifling a giggle.

"Says you. The Archbishop is aware of the original, lewd version."

I exploded again. "He listens to rock and roll?"

"Only, I can assure you, for enlightenment and future guidance. Okay, try *Sh–Boom* and that sacrilegious *Earth Angel*."

"They're okay, but they're still just songs. There's lots of other music being played, like *The Ballad of Davy Crockett*. Does he think that one's bad?"

"Certainly not, but consider please. One vocation from St. Joe's this year. Hundreds of thousands of teenagers whooping it up—and getting away with it. Frankly, I'm puzzled." He stood, knocked on the door, bade goodnight to my mother and left.

I looked at the kitchen clock. Almost eleven. Speed was in order: a quick bath, clothes to the basement, run upstairs, hop into bed and click on the radio. My bedside clock said eleven fifteen. The radio hummed as it warmed. Over background noise the word "sports" came through clearly. Yes, definitely, I was on time.

"And now," the radio announced, "from CKUA, here's Steve Woodman and *All the Best*."

CKUA was Edmonton's least-listened-to station; it was originally a small outlet on the University of Alberta campus and had been moved downtown in an attempt to expand its audience with a format of classical music, jazz, short dramas and talk shows dealing with esoteric subjects. One concession had been made regarding popular music: modern tunes could be aired during the final time slot on the last day of the week. Neither CKUA's position at the extreme end of the radio band nor discriminatory scheduling resulted in Steve being hidden; we kids, compulsive dial spinners, found him. Late Saturday night, CKUA's ratings zoomed.

Most radio stations carried some variation on the top-ten-songs-of-the-week theme. In an era when a piece of music could remain on the charts for months, virtually every other disc jockey demonstrated his boredom by playing a given hit song performed by a different artist from one week to the next. Not Steve: he aired only the best version of the most popular music; anything less, he implied, was equivalent to a grade-school rhythm band trying to imitate an orchestra.

Steve's idea that familiarity bred contentment might have been enough for some listeners but he held his loyal audience with one additional brilliant ploy—his characters. To make the queue of heard-before songs more interesting, the records were introduced either in Steve's voice or in that of a strange, instant person.

I focused the dial and listened; none of the songs could have scandalized the Archbishop. About a quarter to twelve I realized something was happening. Steve was moving along quickly. All the records had been announced normally. Knowing Steve, the unusual was about to occur. *Rock Around the Clock* played. Steve came back on the air.

"Well, I guess that leaves just our number one song to be heard."

From the radio came the sound of a door slamming. A raucous shriek blasted forth.

"Get out of that chair, you young whippersnapper!"

"Hello, Pappy," said Steve to one of his favorite alternate voices. "Isn't it past your bed-time?"

"Yeah, I know," Pappy chortled. "I snuck away when the old lady passed out watching T.V. Guess her eyeballs couldn't stand the exercise. Now get out of here. Go and take a leak or something."

"Pappy," Steve admonished, "you can't say that on the radio."

"Why not?" the voice wheezed. "I brung you a bag of them—leeks, carrots, celery. Take your pick. You like to munch vegetables on your way home don't you? Go on. I've got a goodie for the kids."

"Okay, but remember to lock up, Pappy," said Steve's distant voice as the studio door opened and closed.

Pappy set to work. "Now kids, let's see what Stevie's left me here. I forgot my glasses. The number one record this week is called—gotta squint now—*Jello Grows in Taxis*. That's a new one!"

A martial drum-beat sounded, followed by Mitch Miller's full-throated male choir singing, "There's a yellow rose in Texas, that I am going to zzeep..." The singular sound of a phonograph needle crossing all the remaining grooves split the air. Pappy's cackle came on.

"Hope you were listening real close, kids. I had to play the rest of it fast 'cause I got somethin' else here for you. It's a de-mon-stray-shun record a fella in the States sent up. Got a funny name, Elvis Presley, but he sings real good. Listen."

The new singer rendered a passable version of *The Rock Island Line*. Pappy was back.

"How'd you like that? So-so? Right! But you know what old Pappy went and done? I telephoned long distance—now don't tell anybody, kids—down to the States on the CKUA line and asked some folks there if they had any more songs by this fella. Well, one of them did. He played it for me and he's sending up a copy. Pappy'll run it for you next week. It's called *Blue Moon of Kentucky* and Pappy guarantees it'll rock your socks off."

Midnight. I went downstairs, made a peanut-butter and banana sandwich and ate it eyeing the clock. Upstairs, I brushed my teeth thoroughly and re-entered the bedroom. Twelve-thirty. I would be eligible for communion at Mass that morning. Fasting after midnight was the rule but Edmonton, located half-way across the Mountain Standard Time Zone, had a thirty-five minute reprieve. I settled into bed. Pappy's words blended with Father Fee's as I began to doze. Rock your socks. Rock and roll. Rock around the clock. Rock Island Line. Lots of rocks.

In my drowsy state, I began to chuckle. Christ had said of Saint Peter, "Upon this rock I will build my church." Father Fee said Ape, or Peter as his parents had named him, was the solitary seminarian from our graduating class. I sleepily wondered if the Archbishop was confused as to which rock was to be his church's future foundation.

Music played in my mind and slowly merged with ticking from the bedside clock. I slipped into a satisfied sleep.

We teenagers of the Fifties were a different group: rigidly saluting some institutions after deliberately dismantling others.

2 EARLY IN THE MORNING

In the first minutes of the Fifties I made a decision rather than a New Year's resolution. There were two choices: enter the front door and get my face kissed, or sneak through the back and have a hand crushed. My immediate destination was the hall closet, midway between the vestibule and kitchen. Standing on the sidewalk, I heard *Auld Lang Syne* being pounded on the piano and sung by celebrants. Noisy congratulations were muffled by the glassed-in porch. Mamie Boyle began to thump *It's A Long Way To Tipperary*. The singers were female. Kissing spread polio. The kitchen was safer.

Around back I brushed snow from my moccasins and tried to peek at the partygoers. The outer storm window was clear but the inner pane was steamy; both doors were unlocked. To the left, men with an empty glass in each hand were clustered about stocks of bottles by the sink. On the right, near the stove, my brother-in-law Laval and my step-sister Norine's current boyfriend were engaged in animated discussion. I eased into the kitchen. At age twelve, anonymity was possible in a group of taller adults whose main interest was booze. I edged toward the table. Laval, a former Royal Canadian Air Force fighter pilot, was arguing aerial tactics with Stanislaus. I bent to avoid an elbow in the liquor line. The closet was in sight. My fingers were intact.

Laval spun around. "Attention everyone. I'd like to introduce a new arrival."

The eye-level elbow turned on Laval's command and knocked me sitting onto a chair. I smiled, hands jammed into jacket pockets. Mamie was playing *When Johnny Comes Marching Home*.

"Stan here," Laval continued, "works for Trans-Canada Airlines. Before that, he joined the RAF in England after Poland fell. Stan claims Polish pilots were as good as Canadians during the war."

"Or bedder, old boy." Stan spoke with a curious British-Slavic accent.

Laval was both inebriated and irritated. "Some day, my friend, you go too far."

"We test," said Stan, staggering to the middle of the kitchen. He fashioned a loop on the string leading up to our ceiling light fixture, lifted the small circle above his head and let it fall like a pendulum. "Try to hit it with your finger," he challenged, looking at Laval. "No bending of the arm. No stopping."

Laval charged like a bull and missed by a foot. Stan brushed the string with his sleeve. Laval hit the string but not the loop. Stan did likewise. The game continued until onlookers demanded their turns. Stan and Laval sat across the table from me. Mamie was trilling *The White Cliffs of Dover*.

"Why," asked Stan, as he set his beer down, "does that woman keep singing the war songs? This is a night to be happy."

"She *is* happy," replied Laval. He gave his French-Canadian wink. "The women are still celebrating. They're singing and having babies. The war's over."

Stan glowered. "The war is not over."

"Sure it is. We beat the Nazis and the Japs."

"But we did not beat the Russians."

Laval's eyebrows raised. "You think we should have attacked an ally in 1945?"

"It was in the plans." Stan lowered his voice. "Did you know the German prisoners-of-war were moved around until they got joined with their old units? And did you know guns were made ready to give to them? And were you told the whole western army was on full battle-alert at the end of the war?"

Laval had not left Canada during World War Two. He was amazed. "Where did you get that information?"

"I was there." Stan took a long draught of beer. "If one Russian crossed the line we were ready to smash them." He slammed his empty bottle on the table. "I wish we made the attack. Then I can be in my country now."

"Did you go back after the war?"

"No. When I mustered out of the air force my people in London told me to stay because the Russians killed Polish officers. I checked with relatives and they told me only enlisted men were returning from the eastern front. All the officers were disappeared."

"How about the ones the Germans captured?"

"Those who went home? Disappeared too after a while. Weeks, months, up to a year I wait in London. My people continue to say it is not safe. I come to Canada instead. If I go home, those Communist bastards shoot me."

I parked my jacket in the closet and slipped upstairs past the singers. In bed, I recalled being mystified by the struggle between Nationalists and Communists for control of the Chinese mainland. According to newspaper accounts, the Communists had won. By Stan's reckoning, a new set of bad guys was getting an upper hand in the world.

My apprehension grew in February when newspapers reported the mutual aid treaty signed by China and Russia. Winston Churchill had referred in 1946 to an iron curtain around eastern Europe; magazine columnists added "bamboo curtain" to the nomenclature. Most ominously, radio newscasters hinted Russia was building atomic bombs. Then, on June 25, 1950, Communist North Korea invaded the peninsula's democratic south.

Until this last week of Grade Seven, the St. John's Social Studies program was more concerned with memorizing cabinet ministers' names than with world events. Sister Edwin gave us a crash course on The Cold War.

"You are," she told us, "the first generation in history to reach the age of reason under shadow of a mushroom cloud. You were seven to eight years old when those atomic bombs exploded. You saw the pictures. People in Japan were turned into vapor, leaving only body-shaped outlines on bridges and streets. Now, I fear, the same could happen to you. The war in Korea may be the start of World War Three. Godless Communists have atomic bombs. You might soon be martyrs in heaven. Keep yourselves in a state of grace and pray for the conversion of Russia."

Sister Edwin had faith in the power of prayer; our gang—Ape excepted—did not share her optimism. We gathered on the baseball diamond at recess and pondered the prospect of instant annihilation.

"I'll never sin again," declared Ape, his eyes sinking deeper into their cavernous sockets. "When the bomb falls, I'm going straight to heaven."

"Hell's more likely" replied Red. "Vanity. You just committed a cardinal sin by saying you'll be perfect forever."

"Bull," said Richard. "The best way to get to heaven is to be a martyr, like Sister said. When I grow up, I'm going into the American army, same as my brother." Richard was a Texan whose father had come to Alberta during the Leduc oil boom. The brother was a main source of stamps for my world-wide collection.

I remembered the map on my bedroom wall. "There's no way," I stated, "the Russian planes can get to us without stopping for fuel in the Yukon. They'd have to invade the Northwest Territories first. We'd have lots of warning."

"You ever heard of aircraft carriers?" Robert asked. He was the youngest member of the group and, as I had done before his arrival, carved his niche by being a store of information. I was about to discount the chance of an attack from the Pacific coast.

"Come on, you guys, let's play ball." Mert had a direct approach to problems: ignore them. Current affairs were irrelevant; important events were settled on the playing field.

Robert picked up a baseball bat. "Might as well play now. We won't be here tomorrow. No point in studying any more."

Robert's remark caught my attention. He and I vied for the honors roll at St. John's. If Robert was dropping out of the race, only Pauline and Patsy remained as challengers for the highest average in Grade Seven. I was wondering what the girls were saying when Red interrupted my musings.

"You're right," he muttered. "There'll be plenty of time to get ready. I'm gonna go home and plan the perfect bomb shelter." He drew me aside. "Look at them. Ape: when the bomb goes boom he'll have a second or two to doubt his prayers. Richard: a uniform won't protect him. Robert: standing out in the open saying 'Blow me up.' And Mert: a chalk outline at home plate. You and me, we're survivors. We can figure out how to beat this thing."

After school I surveyed my home. There was a crawl-space under the front porch used for tool storage, but it was at ground level and the walls were wood. The rumpus-room in our basement was better, but its large window would admit the fireball. The best place, away from light and protected by heavy beams, was beneath our cellar stairs. I recalled with some irony that my childhood nemesis—The Beast In The Basement—chose to lurk there; perhaps this secure location was the reason it lived forever.

My basement perusals were noticed. Mother, a former teacher, maintained a keen awareness of the news. Her interest had been practical after my father died—she supplemented a widow's pension with substitute teaching stipends. After her marriage to T.J., the habit of being well-informed persisted. Perceiving my concern, she offered an oblique solution to the nuclear problem; the conversation was so innocuous I did not realize its significance.

"Your step-father and I," she said one July evening, "think you and Mickey would enjoy a vacation in St. Paul. Laval will pick you up on Sunday."

"Do I have to go?" I asked, leaving my nine year old brother to formulate his own arguments.

"Yes. We think you may learn a great deal living a while in a small town. For instance, have you ever fired the rifle your grandfather left you?" When I shook my head she continued, "Laval says the hills and trees in the region are ideal for target-shooting practice. I would be interested in finding out if you inherited Buffalo Bill's prowess."

The mention of grandfather's cousin withered my resistance. I had countless times cocked the rifle, aimed, and triggered the pin forward on an empty chamber. The chance to use bullets was an irresistible challenge and I packed my bags that night.

When Mickey asked, "Are we almost there?" before the Dodge left Edmonton's city limits, Laval drew on his expertise as a courtroom lawyer—he talked.

"We've got over a hundred miles to go. Keep your eyes open for deer. We'll be driving by a fire that never goes out, and the smallest church in the world and, just before St. Paul, you'll see the magnificent twin cities."

As he maintained the patter, I discerned a difference between female and male driving habits. Mother's friends looked at her as they chatted, with occasional glances ahead; Laval maintained a steely stare at the highway while he spoke. T.J., I recalled, did the same. Laval handed me a road map. Mickey watched for wildlife.

Our east-bound car turned north onto a rutted rural road by Mundare. "Shorter this way," said Laval, "but dustier." I looked back; the road was obscured. Laval continued. "Driving is like flying. We practised by pretending clouds were flak bursts. Potholes can shake you up just as much." He guided the car from side to centre to edge of the road; the ride was as smooth as on pavement.

We stopped. Laval rolled down his window and pointed to a field. "What do you see?" He fanned his rugged face with a spotless fedora.

"Cows," said Mickey.

"Stubble burning," I stated in a superior tone.

"Mickey's right and you're wrong," Laval declared. With a wink he added, "I always defend the little guy. Take a closer look. If that's burning stubble, where's the smoke?"

Cattle were grazing at the circumference of a barren circle filled with dozens of flickering flames. The blackness I had seen was soil, not charred vegetation. Tongues of fire danced back and forth among cracks in the ground.

"Natural gas," said Laval. "It lit up when tractors broke the land in the Twenties."

"Why are they wasting it?" I asked. "Can't they snuff it out with a big bell like we use for candles at church? They could leave the snuffer on the ground and run a pipe over to heat the barn in winter."

"Good idea," Laval replied, "and the farmer wanted to do that. However," he sighed, "the province has rights to minerals. If the farmer used the gas he would have to pay huge taxes. There's enough to heat a dozen barns but he can't sell the excess to his neighbors because he doesn't own it. So it just burns off."

"That's dumb," Mickey observed.

"That's government," Laval growled.

The car gunned forward as Laval made up lost time. He appeared to be chewing gum—the muscles in his temple clenched rhythmically. "Some day," he said, "I'm going to run for election." We passed over a crest. "There it is." On the left was a carefully crafted miniature church scarcely large enough to hold four people standing.

"Why's the cross different?" Mickey asked.

"Orthodox." Laval stretched his arms against the steering wheel as we sped along.

"Three generations of Ukrainian people live on that farm. The grandmother is terrified of cars. When *baba's* brittle bones couldn't take the wagon trip to town the priest offered to bring her communion. Not good enough: the old lady said she'd walk to church. So they built her one."

"Why didn't she move to town?" I wondered out loud.

Laval's eyes widened and made a startled dart in my direction. "You have a great deal to learn, my friend. She was forced out of Russia at the turn of the century and no pain would make her leave the land a second time. You ever wondered why the Slavic people fought the Nazis so fiercely?

Someone else was on their land. Buildings were leveled; they could be rebuilt. Crops were burned; they would grow again. But land—that's different. It's home."

I found Laval's statement difficult to understand. Having lived in four houses over almost thirteen years, I thought family and friends more important than front and back yards. The countryside we passed was sparsely populated.

"Do they like land because there aren't many people around?"

"The prosecution has raised an interesting point, m'lord," said Laval, nodding to Mickey. "I request a short recess to consider the issue."

We drove in silence. The car dipped into a broad valley. "North Saskatchewan River, kids. Ahead are the magnificent twin cities of Duvernay and Brosseau."

Clustered on a flatland near the bridge was a miserably tiny collection of shacks and houses; the focal point was a general store *cum* gas station. Across the water a similar ensemble was scattered up a gentle slope.

"Those don't look like cities," Mickey blurted.

"The people consider them cities," said Laval, tapping a forefinger to his temple, "in here." The finger angled in my direction. "Land loses some of its sentimental value if there's nobody to pass it on to. How are you gonna keep 'em down on the farm after they've seen St. Paul? Answer: you make a rivalry between two villages. The farm kids board and do odd jobs here. Everybody keeps track of the census. If a baby's born in Brosseau, somebody creates a job in Duvernay. It is most unpatriotic to leave unless you take agriculture at the university. The understanding is you'll come back. Old people tell young ones that in twenty years their towns will be as big as Edmonton and Strathcona and they'll amalgamate. Land prices will boom and everybody'll be rich.

"They believe that?" I asked.

"They must. They're here. When kids get married they live in town until the parents die or can't work the land alone any more. Then somebody's handy to inherit the farm. It's been very effective."

"I'm hungry," said Mickey, indicating he needed a bathroom stop. Laval pushed the gas pedal.

"Almost home," our brother-in-law declared, pointing at a distant church steeple.

Laval's entry into St. Paul was like a one-car wedding procession: he honked and waved at all passers-by. We turned onto a dirt street and stopped before a small house with brick-patterned asphalt siding. Mickey sped through the front door without knocking. Laval and I gathered the luggage.

"What did you learn today?" he asked.

"How to steer a car around potholes."

Laval's eyes rolled. "*Mon Dieu*! Hasn't anybody told you the difference between training and learning? Driving is training." He picked up the rifle. "Shooting is training. What did you learn?"

"St. Paul is three hours from Edmonton?"

"Not if you walk. Not if you fly." He sat on the Dodge's hood. "Learning isn't this or that precise point—it's about general things going on in the world—like how and why people behave as they do."

"People like to own land?"

"Close. People like to think they own land. They really don't own it—they rent from the government. The yearly rent is the property tax. If the province wants land, all it has to do is raise taxes or expropriate outright. It's a game," he shrugged. "The only people that possess land are the Indians, and even now the Feds try to cheat them out of it." He heaved a suitcase. "One day I shall go to Ottawa and wake everybody up." He laughed as we climbed the stairs. "It bugs me to call some colleague in court 'my learned friend' when I know the guy is just trained and not educated. Today you found out one way people get by is to tell themselves a lie so often they start to believe it. Like that *baba* near Mundare. Convince her on Saturday she doesn't own her land and you'll hear on Sunday she died. By kidding herself, she stays alive."

We paused at the door. Laval looked at me. "While we're on the topic of staying alive, do you know why you were sent here?"

I shook my head.

"Because," Laval whispered, "If the A-bomb falls on Edmonton you won't be there and if the Commies invade," he hefted the rifle, "you'll know how to defend yourself. Your mother is looking out for you the same way British families did when they sent their children to Canada after France fell. If you're alive then no matter what happens to her, she and your late father continue to exist. That, my friend, is another way people cope."

3 RICOCHET

Laval's comments about survival puzzled me: it was unusual for Mother to hint that Michael and I were different from her "six other children." In 1936 she had married a widower with a son—Edward and three daughters—Jean, Patricia and Mary, or Mim, as we called her. I was born in 1937 and Michael arrived three years later. Our father died in 1941. After six years of widowhood Mother married T.J., a widower with two grown children—Patrick and Norine. I therefore had a brother, half-brother, step brother, three half-sisters and one step-sister. I wondered, if nuclear war was imminent, why Mother had chosen our half-sister to look after us.

Norine had an apartment three blocks away, so staying with her made no sense. Patrick lived in Saskatoon; if small prairie cities like Edmonton were at risk, his home was not safe. Edward worked in Sudbury; nickel mines could be pivotal in a war. Mim was in New York—another obvious target. Jean, out of the line of fire in Brisbane, Australia, would have been the most logical choice but a move there constituted extreme reaction. Mother was not one to panic and had picked Patricia, I reasoned, because the threat needed time for assessment: perhaps atomic destruction was not a certainty.

My relief was brief: during supper Laval extolled St. Paul's role as an agricultural, trade and transportation centre. The town, he implied, was a key cog in the machinery running Western Canada. I had a mental image of a Kremlin map with St. Paul as the bull's eye. Patricia brought me back to reality as we stacked plates in the sink.

"Don't bother helping," she said, tilting her blonde head toward Laval's feet on the chesterfield. "His nibs wants to show you and Mickey our five strategic grain elevators."

"Do the dishes," came a muffled response from the living room. "The tour's on for tomorrow. You forgot to tell them about our main street."

"I didn't want the thrill to be too great," Pat replied.

"One street?" Mickey asked.

"Try to look impressed," Pat whispered.

The next morning I had further reason to doubt St. Paul's importance. Mickey, not wasting jaw movements, talked as he ate breakfast. "The toilet sounds funny." My brother had a disconcerting habit of raising distasteful subjects at meal-time.

"The honey bucket's probably full." Laval sounded annoyed.

"Honey?" Mickey halted his bread knife's progress toward the jam tin.

"Eat," ordered Pat, "while you still have your appetite."

While Mickey munched, Laval slowly mopped egg yolk with his last bite of toast. Looking at the brown and black crust, our brother-in-law gulped, dropped the yellow-streaked specimen on his plate and charged to the bathroom. He emerged in a running stagger, an oblong bucket held at arms-length. Pat held the back door open and Laval lunged toward a wood outhouse by the lane.

"We've got water," Pat explained, "but no sewage. The chemical toilet's a step along the road to civilization, but sometimes..." she paused expectantly as Laval opened the outside faucet, hosed the pail, got sprayed and cursed, "...it brings forth the savage in him."

When Laval walked downtown with Mickey and me, I understood one reason he worked in St. Paul: a lawyer was a celebrity. He greeted everyone on a first-name basis—with one exception.

"Mrs. Poloway," Laval exclaimed with unusual deference. "I'd like Patricia's brothers to have the pleasure of meeting you."

I wiped a sweaty palm on my pants and grasped four flaccid fingers. The day was sunny and warm, the lady sullen and cool.

"You are from the city? It is good. There are fewer temptations in a town."

"Temptations?" Laval scoffed. "The only sin around here is my Wednesday afternoon poker game. Can Orest come?"

"My husband," the woman replied icily, "will be in the Bonnyville area all week and unavailable."

Laval glanced over his shoulder as Mrs. Poloway entered the Marshall-Wells hardware store. He clapped his hands. "Hot damn! The coast is clear. She's the game warden's wife. We go hunting today by St. Brides."

"Where's that?" asked Mickey.

"West of here," Laval grinned. "Bonnyville is east. Orest's wife doesn't approve of gambling and keeps quiet about my invitations. I always know where he's patrolling except," he winked, "during hunting season—then it's safe."

"We're gonna poach?" I said loudly. A pedestrian raised his eyebrows. Laval raised his voice.

"Yep. And fry and scramble and hard-boil all those eggs you brought from Edmonton." He gazed after the man, who did not break stride. "Watch it. Gossip travels fast. We don't want to end up in jail."

Mickey tensed. "Jail?"

"At Fort Saskatchewan," Laval said nonchalantly. "It's close to Edmonton, so your mother can visit you once a week."

I choked. "Are you sure shooting's okay?"

Laval warmed to the tease. "But yes. If we're caught, jail's a great place to see famous people. Hollywood makes lots of prison movies and you might meet Humphrey Bogart or George Raft. Do you know my sister met Bing Crosby?"

"In jail?" Mickey asked.

"No, at the Jasper Park Lodge. Bing was in the mountains touring and golfing. After a couple of weeks he asked his caddy if there were any more local attractions. Blanche got dragged out from the Lodge kitchen. After considerable coaxing she licked her nose. Bing said she was the eighth wonder of the world and gave her a silver dollar. My sister," Laval shrugged, "spent it."

The mention of money triggered our brother-in-law into a buying frenzy. We criss-crossed the street purchasing cowboy apparel. "It's good for business," the lawyer remarked as we entered the fourth store, "to spread the spending."

As we shopped I was surprised by similarities between St. Paul and Edmonton—the difference was in scale. Where city stores had a dozen identical items per shelf, the town's businesses stocked two or three. Main Street had Jasper Avenue's variety of services without the city's redundancy of buildings. I also noticed St. Paul's merchants did not abuse their monopoly: courteous attention from salespeople was a new experience. Stetsons fitted exactly. Iridescent neckerchiefs matched our hat bands. Large-buckled cowboy belts felt comfortable when we hitched our jeans. The pervasive feeling was one of honor. Reputation, I deduced, was important in a small town.

Mickey looked pleased with his new gunslinger identity; I felt conspicuous and wondered about Laval's judgement: the western garb pointed straight at our supposedly secret expedition.

"Do we need all this to go hunting?"

Laval lowered his hands to his knees. Our eyes were level. "Get one thing straight, my friend. You and Mickey are outsiders here. Strangers are regarded with suspicion. The quickest way to get accepted is to become part of the town. The outfit you wear is an advertisement for the approaching St. Paul Stampede."

"Stampede?" Mickey blurted, "Like Calgary's?"

"Just the same, only smaller. Look," Laval said, reading doubt on my face, "I'll prove you've become citizens."

We entered the Imperial Oil service station. Laval exchanged greetings with the owner. "Patricia's brother," I overheard, "had to give up his paper route when he came to visit. Could you find him a job for a couple of weeks?"

The owner approached. T.J. had taught me how to shake hands. "Good firm grip," Mr. Tannous observed. "You're hired." He glanced at his garage. "A cowpoke starts by cleaning stables and..." I followed his gaze to the gasoline pumps, "...works up to feeding the horses."

"In St. Paul," Laval said contentedly as we ambled home, "you've got two thousand kinfolk."

"Even the game warden?" I asked.

"Every family," Laval grimaced, "has a black sheep."

I became restless after lunch. At three-thirty I learned we'd be hunting upland game. Our guns were oiled and ready. At twenty to four I aimed grandfather's rifle toward the clock and imagined my bullets leading a wing of geese. Our ammunition, boxed and stacked, sat on a coffee table. One shell had failed inspection. "Bent cartridges," Laval stated, "are only good for shooting around corners." The last direct beam of sunlight eased across the living-room floor. We had supper.

"Why're we waiting?" Mickey fidgeted.

Laval was relaxed. "The game will be hungry soon. In autumn grain trucks hit the valley potholes. The bird's dinner gets shaken out. Grouse and partridge have long memories and they search the road all summer, but just at twilight and dawn."

"Less traffic?" I asked.

Laval laughed. "No, because their enemies, the hawks, are full of mice in the evening and sleep late in the morning."

We got in the car, turned a corner and entered the countryside.

I looked across a small lake. "There's some ducks!"

"They're not in season. The farmers don't mind if an occasional prairie chicken is shot—they can be as bad as crows picking a crop clean—but ducks could be part of the poultry stock. Those," he gestered with his thumb, "are mud hens. Taste awful."

"Besides," I added knowingly, "the bullet could go across the lake and hit a cow or something."

Laval braked the car so violently I thought we had hit a tree.

"Have you, my young friend, ever shot that gun?"

"No," I replied.

"I thought not." He geared into reverse and stopped by the water. "Take your rifle, aim straight at those ducks and fire away."

I was worried. Laval had *ordered* me to shoot. If I did not bag a duck, he implied, the hunting trip was over. I loaded the gun and firmed my feet on the beach. The tiny figures bobbed slightly. I waited until the ducks formed a cluster halved by the gunsight. Rifle steady. Trigger squeezed. Shoulder hit by recoil. Ducks undisturbed. The bullet had splashed nearer to us than the prey.

"That," Laval said, pointing at the widening circles on the water, "is called the drop. The farther the target, the higher you have to aim. When you wondered about hitting a cow, I got the impression you think a bullet goes on forever. Even to the moon sometimes?" The thought had crossed my mind but I was too embarrassed to speak. Laval chuckled. "I dreamed the same when I was your age. Let's go to the place where my father taught me to shoot."

We walked along the shore to a sand hill. The steep slope faced west. Sunlight gave the multicolored sand the appearance of stucco. "Broken bottles," Laval observed with satisfaction. "They're still using it." I had been preoccupied with carrying my gun safely and had not noticed Laval's cargo: a beer case.

Laval went to the dune and set twelve bottles in a clock-face pattern. We retreated to a small meadow. "This spot," Laval stated, "is exactly one hundred yards from the cliff. Watch while I aim at the clock's centre."

He shot. A puff of dust appeared above six o'clock. "That's the drop from this distance. Try it."

Mickey and I took turns. To my chagrin, little brother's bullets landed in the circle while mine strayed left. I licked my finger: there was no wind. Laval seemed amused.

"You can't blame the breeze. Look at the clock with both eyes and cover the middle with that wet finger. Close your right eye. Is the finger on or off centre?"

"On," I sputtered angrily.

"Now open your right eye and close the left."

"Off," I marvelled. "Way off."

"Close your right eye when you shoot. Now," he said as I aimed, "take out nine o'clock."

I fired. The bottle shattered. Laval called random numbers. The last bottle exploded.

"Twelve bullets," Laval whistled. "You, sir, are deadly."

On the way home past St. Brides, Laval dispatched six partridge with his double-barrelled shotgun. He skinned and cleaned the birds at roadside so the victims would be anonymous—should Orest happen by.

I was calm and confident. If we were invaded I need not wait until "the whites of their eyes" were visible: my firing range had expanded tenfold. Perhaps Richard had the right idea: a rifle, though no match for an atomic bomb, was better than nothing.

"Quick," Patricia motioned as we entered the house, "your mother's on the line."

Mickey grabbed the telephone; Laval, anticipating something, stood rudely close to him. While my brother chattered, my brother-in-law's hand edged toward the receiver.

"Yep," Mickey said, "we went hunting and got six prairie chicken."

Laval's arm lashed like a snake. "Florence," he purred, "your city-bred boy has a wild imagination. We got six sparrows this evening. They're bigger up here, Billy says." Laval slumped on the sofa. "Over to you," he whispered, "and remember, you're talking on a party line. Jail," the word rumbled, "is only a slip of the tongue away."

"Hi, Mom, we shot some sparrows today," I quivered as Laval nodded. "We're going to eat them tomorrow."

Morning dew glistened on the fuel pumps. A mechanic let me in the shop. I found a push-broom and began to sweep. When Mr. Tannous arrived, the parking area was clear of gravel and my palms were beginning to blister.

"Good job," the owner smiled approvingly. "You wash car windows. I pump gasoline." Loud cursing preceded our first customers' arrival. A driverless yellow Packard, dusty and dented, coasted onto the pavement. Two sweating inebriated youths lay gasping on the trunk; another was collapsed in the front seat, his limp arm entwined in the steering wheel.

"Fill 'er up," ordered a female voice from the floor. I looked through the window. The teenage girl was naked. "Not me," she said, trying to uncross her eyes, "I'm full." My face blushed so rapidly it hurt.

I averted my gaze, almost, while washing the front and side windows twice. Catholic churches usually heard confessions Saturday afternoon and this was Tuesday: I could live in mortal sin four days. But diligent work was a virtue and a thorough job on the bug-spattered glass seemed in order. Mr. Tannous took the scenario serenely as he concentrated on the hose nozzle. The pump dials whirred longer than expected. A pool of rainbow fluid appeared beneath the car and meandered to the street.

"Mr. Tannous," I shouted, "the tank's full."

The boss scowled. "Do your job. It still sounds hollow."

The flow of fuel became a torrent. I stepped aside.

"What's wrong with you, boy?"

"It's pouring out, sir."

Our eyes met behind the rear wheels. The gas tank was a sieve —two streams and three trickles splashed on the pavement.

Mr. Tannous stood and froze: one trunk-pusher was lighting a cigarette; his boozy hand waved the flaming match to the cement. Mr. Tannous stomped the fire with a standing broad-jump that belied his grey hair.

"You've got a leak," he growled.

"We've all gotta leak," a voice from the front seat giggled. "You got rest-rooms here?"

Mr. Tannous pointed a trembling finger east. "Pay up and piss off."

A five-dollar bill fluttered in the air. "Keep the change," yelled a youth as he piled in the back seat. The engine's sound was obscured by whoops as the vehicle roared off. I watched the car lose speed. Two figures rolled out and shoved the Packard into a station three blocks away; I wondered if an exploding yellow car would resemble the Shell logo. The automobile, freshly fueled, again shot eastward and was gone when the dust settled.

"Who are those guys?"

"They *were* local boys," said Mr. Tannous. He stared at the face on the fiver. "For King and Country they joined the army. Wanta go to Korea. Prob'ly be there by Christmas. Prob'ly be dead by spring." He folded the bank note and pocketed it. "I'll have Father Giroux say a mass for them on Sunday."

St. Paul, I discovered, during exploratory walks, was a combination of wood shacks and neat frame houses, false-front trading posts and whitewashed modern stores. In contrast with the residential and commercial areas, the church was magnificent: I had seen nothing like it in Edmonton. The soaring spire topped with a cross centred a brick building embellished with stained glass windows. Inside, I tiptoed awe-struck past orderly pews facing an ornate altar. I paused at the communion rail longing for a closer look since walking in the sanctuary was barred to the laity.

A priest was patrolling the side aisle, reading his breviary.

"Pardon me, Father," I said, waiting until he had flipped a colored tassel to the next section of his prayerbook. "May I serve Mass on Sunday?"

The young priest paused and smiled. "O Lord, hear my prayer."

"*Et clamor meus ad te veniat*," I replied.

"Which translates as...?"

"And let my cry come unto Thee."

"Request granted. Nine o'clock tomorrow."

I detoured to a confessional on the way out. One advantage of the Catholic penitential sacrament was that you did not have to go into lurid detail. The gas station incident was disguised as "two impure thoughts"—the observation itself and my recalling *with regret* I had forgotten to dust the dashboard.

Having had my soul cleansed or, as T.J. was fond of saying, my pot scoured, I felt ready for Sunday morning.

The cathedral is full. Low Mass. No singing. Priest rumbles in Latin. Congregation responds with kneeling, standing, genuflecting and sitting. They don't speak. I answer in Latin for them. A stranger has usurped their church. I begin to feel smug, faintly superior. The priest's left hand flicks to the altar. He has reached the epistle's last paragraph. I take the cue to move the missal. Descend the altar steps and avoid communion bells. Genuflect. Ascend without tripping on my cassock. Flawless. I wait. Priest approaches. Turns page. Puts thumb to his forehead and makes a small cross. I do the same. Perfect. Then a ripple of cold passes down my neck. Something's different. The people rise like a disciplined army. No premature jumping-jacks. No laggards. They stand for the gospel as one. They and the priest are saying Mass. I'm doing their servile work. Instant humility. I blush. Priest senses my sag. Deviates from the text.

"Welcome to St. Paul, my son."

4   BLUEBERRY HILL

During the gospel reading I was uncomfortable. A familiar feeling had settled, like a butterfly, on the back of my head. I knew what the sensation meant: my subconscious was telling me there was something I should remember. Brushing a hand across my hair never dislodged the butterfly—it would leave only if I recalled the elusive memory.

The first time I had recognized the feeling and asked my mother about it, she shampooed me. Still curious, and marshalling my then five-year-old vocabulary for maximum clarity, I had gone to Mim.

"How do you know when you've forgot?"

Mim was amused. "Your mother reminds me."

"No, I mean when you're coming home from the store and you forgot to get carrots."

"*Before* you match the groceries against the list?"

"Yah." I described the butterfly feeling. Mim didn't laugh.

"I think everybody gets it. My 'butterfly' lands here," she said, pointing above her right eye. "It came one night when a bunch of us girls tried to remember a boy's name. I noticed everyone scratching the same place. You feel it at the back?"

"Near the top."

"Pay attention because it's handy. I always check my forehead when I've finished shopping or start out on a date. Sometimes, when I finally remember, the butterfly goes straight to my tummy."

The priest came back from the pulpit. In preparation for the mid-Credo genuflection, his congregation toed down their kneelers. The sound resembled scouts slamming wood staves to attention on the St. John's gymnasium floor. My scout troop and this congregation were similar. The butterfly began to leave.

I stood with the priest at the altar. A scout army was schooled in worldly survival; the church militia, expecting atomic war, was preparing for heaven. Was I safest in the church? No, the butterfly had settled down again. Was I better off in the countryside, using my rifle and scout wilderness training? Yes, said the butterfly as it departed.

Unlike me, some people in town seemed determined to die prematurely—they lined up to ride bulls and broncs at the St. Paul Stampede.

Mother and T.J. drove out on the fair's final day. We sat in the stands watching wild horses toss spurred riders skyward. I saw blood on one stallion's flank. Laval appeared.

"Enjoying the show?" he asked.

"I'm not sure Michael should be watching this," said Mother, nodding toward my little brother.

"Nonsense," replied Laval, "it's good fun. A few people get maimed for life and some get killed. The show goes on. Great entertainment. I brought the boys hot dogs."

I looked at red ketchup flanking the wiener and traded with Mickey. "I'll take the one with the mustard."

Mickey stared at my lunch. "If they made wieners out of caterpillars, all you'd have to do is squeeze them and the mustard would pop out." With that, he ate his hot dog—and mine.

Mother wanted to leave. "Don't worry," T.J. reassured her, "lawyers are ninety per cent bull and ten per cent fact."

"THE NEXT EVENT IS BULL RIDING," the announcer intoned, like an undertaker giving news of a pending funeral. I looked for Laval. He had materialized by the chutes. T.J. was right.

The first bull, named Tornado, charged from the pen, whirled its rider off with one twist, stomped him with four hooves and impaled the cowboy on the ground with a fearsome pair of horns. The goring stopped when rodeo clowns spun and jumped to distract the beast. Trained horses guided Tornado to an exit gate. The crowd was silent. A first-aid crew with Red Cross armbands swarmed around the rider. The twitching body was lifted on a stretcher and eased out of the corral. Mother was pale. The announcer cleared his throat. I looked over. He had a sheet of paper.

"MICHAEL O'CALLAGHAN, GET READY FOR YOUR STEER."

We drove to Edmonton that night.

"Got an early train to catch," T.J. said. "Postal convention's in Toronto this year. Four days on the rails. Want to ride in the cattle car, Mickey?"

Mother was not amused.

I was concerned. We were heading, with Mother's approval, to a more inviting wartime target than either Edmonton or St. Paul. The capital of Ontario. Half a million people. Industries. A National Hockey League team. Altogether, certain atomic bomb-bait.

"How long are we staying there?" I asked.

"A day or so," Mother replied, "then you'll be staying with Mim for a week."

New York? Eight million people. The business centre of North America. One hockey team and *three* baseball teams. Had my parents surrendered to the inevitable?

Mickey sat up. "Can we see the Brooklyn Dodgers?"

Mother shook her head. "I don't think so. Mim lives in Syracuse."

"Where's Syracuse?" I imagined a suburb like Jasper Place or St. Albert.

"In upstate New York," Mother answered. "It's two hundred miles from the Dodgers and," she nodded in my direction, "the Yankees."

I relaxed.

The next morning we boarded a Canadian National Railways coach. A Negro porter led us to our roomettes. Mickey charged through the door on the right and hit the window. We would, I saw, be spending four days in a closet. Behind the door was a toilet; near the window stood a small metal sink; on the opposite side lay a padded bench. The narrow walkway did not allow us to stand shoulder-to-shoulder. The train shuddered. I looked out the window over Mickey's head. A line of freight cars beside us shifted left. We were on our way.

I thought. Mickey spoke. Same topic.

"Maybe we should check the biffy." He did not want to live four days in a gradually filling outhouse.

I paused. A small sign declared: *Do not flush toilet when train is in station.* We eased out of the rail yards. I lowered the handle. Water fell away. I kept the lever down, peered through the hole, and saw railroad ties and the gravel bed passing slowly below; it would be prudent to jump from steel to steel when crossing CNR tracks in the future.

I was hungry and counted my money. Mr. Tannous had been generous: garage work paid much better than the paper route. My only encounter with railroad food, on Canadian Pacific trips to the lake, led me to believe we had to exist on oranges, soda pop and "sand-wee-jes" flogged by a newsy. T.J. had mentioned his intention to sleep through the entire trip. I counted again. Twenty dollars for Mickey's and my twenty-four meals. More than enough.

A knock sounded. "First call."

Mickey dropped his comic and opened the door. "For what?"

"Lunch time in the dining car. Wash your face and hands so your mother and father don't send you back. We've got a treat today," the voice said. "Seafood caught near my home."

I assumed Mickey was speaking to the conductor but when the train jolted I saw a black hand steady itself on the door frame. I was amazed—the porter did not have a southern accent.

"All you got is fish?" Mickey's voice had a hint of apprehension.

The porter came into full view and smiled. "Have you," he asked Mickey's bobbing head as the train passed over a bridge, "ever tasted Nova Scotia salmon?"

"Sure," my brother said, "after Mom opens the can and picks out the bones and skin."

"I'm certain," replied the porter, as he pursed his lips and chose his words carefully, "your mother makes it taste really good, but you should see what salmon is like *before* the canners get to it. And by the way," he added, "don't drink the malted milk."

On our trek to the diner we resembled pinballs propelled by flipper-like pressurized doors. T.J. blazed the trail with his bare hands: he marked our path by flattening the felt nap on seat backs exposed by children, short men and women with small hats.

I lagged behind, lingering on the shifting steel platforms that covered the cars' coupling locks. Rolling metal plates and rocking train carriages had, when combined with rhythmic clicking from the rails beneath, a soothing, almost sensuous quality. I planted my feet squarely when walking between the cars: an image of being splashed like a bug on the speeding train's doors kept me cautious. The combination of sensual excitement and imminent danger made me extraordinarily alert.

But not alert enough.

"We've ordered for you," Mother said, as I lifted the linen tablecloth and wriggled into my chair. Outside, telephone poles flipped by, farms eased along and distant clouds moved hardly at all.

My silverware clanked. Lunch had arrived. I looked at the plate. Salmon. I teased an edge off the grey-pink oval. It was glutinous. It melted. Totally delicious. The salmon disappeared. The porter was right.

Our waiter poured coffee for T.J., tea for Mother and a light-brown liquid for Mickey and me.

"Chocolate milk?" asked my brother.

"Malted milk," replied the teenager. "It's sweet."

Mickey inhaled his glass. I had half of mine. The fluid had a strange after-taste.

Dessert came. British Columbia cherries—halved and pitted. In cream. Dusted with sugar. Gone.

We waddled forward to our compartment. Mickey lay down to sleep. I watched the countryside. Tree clusters became smaller. We entered the wide prairie. Grain fields stretched unbroken to the horizon. Fencelines blurred. I felt queasy and looked away from the window.

"First call," said a voice outside the door.

Mickey's knees were on his chest. "I'm not hungry," he winced. We excused ourselves from supper.

T.J. said we had motion sickness and tipped the porter to put us to bed. Mickey stood, heaved convulsively and staggered to the toilet. Violent vomiting seemed to shorten his legs. Our porter divined the bowl's contents.

"You had the malted milk," he stated.

I nodded. "The waiter said it was sweet."

"Blond guy? Pimples? British accent?"

I nodded again.

"That's Eric. He tried to warn you. In England, 'sweet' sometimes means rotten. The stuff went bad in Vancouver and the steward's been trying to get rid of it. Double benefit for the railway: no loss on the milk and savings on missed meals. Things like this make me glad I'm going to law school this fall." He motioned. "You're next. Get it over with. Chuck up now and you sleep in a clean bed tonight."

I was dubious but followed his finger to the unflushed toilet.

"Lean over and take a deep breath."

A noxious odor coated my nose and throat. A firm hand pressed my abdomen. Clotted malted milk made an effortless exit. The porter checked the bowl and made a rapid calculation.

"You had less of it." He drew down the upper bunk. "You're up here tonight. The little guy will need another trip or two. I'll leave the night light on."

Our medic's prediction was accurate: Mickey dashed twice to the vomitory; I stayed in bed.

The soft mattress folded around me. My pillow was perfect. I dreamed of water. Lakes and streams glistened but I was unable to move toward them. I awoke. The train had stopped.

My tongue, teeth and lips were dried together. Terminal thirst. Like a needle on a compass, my head swivelled downward to the faucet buttons; feeling snout-stretched into collie form, I followed their magnetic pull to the sink.

At such times, cold water has a startling flavor resembling flat ginger ale. I poured another sip into the conical paper cup, squatted, and raised the window blind.

Midnight mist swirled gently around and among two rows of sentinel lamps fading and shortening into the darkness. A town's main street. No cars. No people. As uninhabited as an airport runway. The prairie fog revealed and covered again small shops and secure homes. Distant windows shone through the haze. Another St. Paul. One of hundreds. Rural havens, unchanging and safe. I returned to my berth.

"Second call."

Mickey tumbled out of bed and opened the door. "Breakfast?" he asked.

"Nope," said the black head which materialized three feet above my brother's shoulders, "it's lunch time."

I unglued my eyelids. "More malted milk?"

"Not a chance," replied the porter. "I chatted with your father after breakfast. Found out he's a post office inspector. I passed the word to Eric that a federal government investigator's on the train."

"So?" I wondered aloud.

"Eric talked to the conductor and had him warn the steward. I think you're in for extra-special treatment. A fact of life," he said, looking mischievously around the ceiling, "is that bad news gets magnified by each person telling it."

Service during lunch was impeccable. The steward himself attended our table. He bowed fulsomely as T.J. stood to leave.

"I hope Your Lordship found the meal satisfactory."

"Quite," said T.J. somewhat bemused.

"Why'd you call him that," asked Mickey, reaching for an extra after-dinner mint after T.J. and Mother left.

"You should know," the steward sniffed, "the proper manner to address the Chief Justice of the Supreme Court."

I told our porter about the incident: he was extraordinarily cheerful for the rest of the day—in contrast with his glowering mood the next morning.

"Derailment up ahead," he warned.

The golden wheat fields and deep black soil of Manitoba had merged into the dark green forest and grey bedrock of Northern Ontario. Our train shuffled, bumped and halted near a small, hilly meadow. We joined the crowd and debarked our grounded schooner. The steward was scurrying about, brushing short foliage with his hand. He approached T.J.

"Just for you, sir," he said obsequiously, "I will prepare these luscious blueberries for your table tonight."

I felt my nausea returning.

"Also," he fawned, "I will pick enough for your wife and sons to dine upon."

A bitter water brash touched my tongue.

"Our train," the steward simpered, "never stops here and this fruit," he added redundantly, "hasn't been picked before."

I imagined blueberries amply fertilized by bouncing poop from the steward's speeding train and declined dessert that night.

The engineer's effort to regain lost time jiggled me awake. The eastern sky had a deep orange glow. The view from our window was not like a motion picture: the rock-tree-lake repetition was similar to a cheaply made cartoon with a magic-lantern, revolving background. Mickey roused and we wandered along the swaying corridor. Our porter was at work.

"Hi, Edwin," Mickey said. Light from the curtained compartment's small bulb reflected off a neatly spaced row of shoes.

"Hungry?" the porter asked, deftly wiggling an oxford's tongue. We shook our heads. "Eric says you missed the fun last night. Did your mother tell you?"

"Nope. What fun?" I asked.

"Some of your father's blueberries," Edwin chuckled, "tried to swim upstream."

"Huh?" we grunted in unison.

"Teeny, tiny worms turned the berries into little motorboats. Your mother noticed it and your father told the steward. Last report Eric gave was the steward sitting and looking longingly at a row of steak knives."

"Edwin?" Mickey's naive questioning tone sent me edging toward the doorway. I cringed as my brother persisted. "How come your hands are white?"

Edwin was not offended, although his brush paused in mid-stroke. He grinned and resumed a slow, careful polish on the shoe's heel. "What happens," he asked, "when you sit out in the sun?"

"I get tanned," Mickey answered.

"Are you any different when you get darker?"

"No," my brother replied.

"Do you think shining these shoes wears away the tan and makes my hands lighter?"

"Yep," said Mickey confidently.

"So you're saying the more I do, the whiter I get?"

I was trying to dissolve in the passageway but someone had to yank Mickey's arm. He avoided my grasp.

"Sure, Edwin. If I lie out in the sun and you keep on working, we'll end up the same."

Edwin beckoned me into the cubbyhole. "Your brother said something you should remember. To get equal, people like me have to try twice as hard. But," his shoulders sagged, "you can't really understand."

I recounted fighting my way to a Catholic school in a predominantly Protestant neighborhood. Edwin recanted.

"Not as obvious," he said, "but the same battle. Going to Toronto? Keep your eyes and ears open. I'll bet you learn how *they* try to push you around."

Edwin was prophetic. We toted our bags to the hotel near the CNR station and dropped them at the front desk.

"Reilly," T.J. said. "Postal Convention. Bedroom suite."

"Very good sir," the desk clerk answered neutrally. He suddenly became animated. "Here are some brochures outlining our tourist attractions. We also have a church directory listing Sunday services. May I assist you? Which will you be attending?"

"Catholic," replied T.J. There was a gleam in his eyes I hadn't seen before.

"Right there," bubbled the clerk. "On-the-hour from nine o'clock Sunday." He turned to the pigeon-hole board behind the desk, searched an inordinate time, and returned. "I'm sorry, we're overbooked. Some of our guests stayed late. All we have is a double. I'm sure you'll find it comfortable." His palm moved to the right but T.J.'s hand had the bell covered.

My stepfather was formidable when furious.

"The chairs in this lobby," he remarked casually, "need reupholstering. Your hide would nicely cover that divan over there. Do you have a telephone handy? I'd like to call Louis St. Laurent."

"The Prime Minister?" choked the functionary.

"The same," growled T.J. "I will not see my family in cramped quarters."

The clerk made a show of recognizing Mother, Mickey and me. "A thousand pardons, sir. I thought you were alone. Let me check once more."

We got our suite.

5 HOW HIGH THE MOON

Toronto's subway was under construction and Mickey and I stood near the guard rail. Thick wood beams covered Front Street and muffled the noise of subterranean digging; I overheard a conversation between two portly businessmen.

"Damned nuisance," said one. "This mess has ruined sales."

"Look at it positively," the other replied. "When those Russkie planes attack, you'll have a ready-made bomb shelter beside your store."

I gazed around and became aware of a strange phenomenon.The city's colors were fading—first to black-and-white and then, gradually, into the brownish hues of an old photograph. For the first time in my life I was experiencing depression. The second man had spoken with authority: war was coming. My life would be finished before my thirteenth birthday. I stared at the sidewalk. Engineered earthquakes vibrating the cement had formed an arrow-shaped crack in the concrete. The arrow pointed west. I wanted to get away. Fast.

"Hi, fellers." Mim's voice. I turned and saw her brilliant blue stewardess uniform with sunlight reflecting off golden buttons and the prominent wing-shaped pin. Yellow braid flashed as her arms encircled us. "Pack your bags. We're flying out today."

Mim. Salvation. The city's rainbow sparkled again.

Our plane's propellers were being tested and the aircraft's clenched-claw wheels rolled against small, triangular blocks; the eagle was straining to fly. Neither Mickey nor I had flown before.

Engines roared. Wings shuddered. Seats thrust forward. Earth receded. Clouds passed. Mim was in the aisle.

"Want to meet the pilot?"

Turbulence rocked the aircraft and I steadied my arms behind the captain's chair. A fluffy panorama floated past below us. I could see the curve of the horizon. The captain read my mind.

"I haven't," he said, "ever hit cloud castles."

Mickey had a firm grip on my shirt. "Does the moon look bigger up here?"

"Nope," replied the pilot. "There's less air to act as a magnifying glass so it actually looks smaller." He turned to his right. "The moon's shrunk! Call in the cavalry."

The co-pilot lifted his microphone. "Toronto to Syracuse. Colonial Airlines. Scramble."

Our captain and his assistant were, I reasoned, quite demented. Horses? Three miles above the ground? I spun around. My head hit Mim's belt buckle. Mickey had also sensed disaster: his fleeing elbow punched my chest. Mim stood firm.

"Hang on," she said, "and watch."

I eased forward. The pilot's eyes were darting back and forth. The co-pilot's head was swinging like a pendulum. The dash dials didn't move. The pilot's eyes clicked ahead.

"Bandits at ten o'clock."

"More bandits at two o'clock," answered the co-pilot.

Mim's hand pressed my shoulder in a hard-soft counting sequence. "All bandits," she said quietly, "are now at twelve o'clock high."

I looked across our bow. Nothing—for a few seconds.

The sky exploded. Jet fighters roared past in a blazing blur. I blinked. The dotted V-wing swept over distant cloudbanks and circled to attack again. The captain raised his speaker.

"Exercise complete. Airliner needs new paint job. Next time, suggest your pilots purchase Colonial tickets before boarding."

Mim guided us to our seats. "Where there's no radar, we have ground observers and aircraft crews keeping watch. Bad guys trying to sneak in," she whispered, "would be shot down by now."

I believed her. Awesome strength. Marshalled in minutes. I relaxed. America was secure territory.

Syracuse had to be older than Edmonton—its boulevard trees were larger. And each house sported what looked like a spiked, old-fashioned lightning rod or weather vane.

"Television antennas," Mim explained. "Mrs. H. has a TV. We'll visit her after supper."

Grace Haines introduced herself as "Grass Hans". Mim had compromised in the battle with upstate New York's A-flattening accent: Mrs. Haines-Hans became "Mrs. H."

A radio sat flush against the living-room's darkest wall. On the console's face a row of dials separated glass circle above from felt rectangle below. I did not realize the appliance was a television set until Mrs. H., gently prodded by Mim's mention that Mickey and I had never seen TV, stood and fiddled the dials. She stepped away with a flourish.

An extraordinarily fat announcer, with vocal resonance befitting an opera baritone, told us the FBI had arrested several communist spies near Washington. Mrs. H. busied herself behind the TV. The announcer slimmed in a snap. A map of Korea appeared. The war was not going well. United Nations troops had been pushed into a small square of territory near Pusan. President Truman was concerned. The weather tomorrow would be sunny and warm.

I was both intrigued and annoyed: technology sent pictures through the air; the image was grainy and distorted. I had seen better definition on the video juke-box at Love's Delicatessen back home in 1945.

Mim sensed the invisible vibrations which join blood relatives. "It gets better at eight. You'll see Ed Sullivan's *Toast Of The Town*." Ed was on holidays. A guest host did the show. Mim apologized. "I guess you're not impressed."

I nodded in agreement. Black-and-white television did not challenge technicolor movies.

Mrs. H. turned a dial. Mickey stared at the screen's bright, receding dot; he jumped when Mrs. H. snapped her fingers.

"Hah," she exclaimed. "The boy got hypnotized. TV does that to you. When I found myself studying the test pattern long past midnight, I decided to mark the newspaper for programs worth watching. Then I set the alarm clock. Otherwise," she said, collapsing into her armchair, "I'd squat here and starve to death."

The next day Mim borrowed Mrs. Haines' car and we toured the city. Syracuse had a strong resemblance to Edmonton—with one major exception: Tipperary Hill. We drove to the crest, edged to the curb and parked in an elm tree's shade.

"Notice anything different?" Mim asked.

I looked at the signs surrounding the square. O'Flaherty's Flowers. Casey's Groceries. Dunnigan's Garage. Hoolihan's Hardware. "The stores all have Irish names."

Mickey was more observant. "The traffic light," he stated, "is upside down."

Mim's hand thumped the steering wheel. "You got it," she laughed. "For two years the Syracuse Police Department wondered why the orange light kept getting shot out. Finally," she giggled, "somebody suggested putting the green *above* the orange. Tipperary Hill's been peaceful ever since."

When the airliner back to Toronto wasn't buzzed by jet fighters, I became apprehensive. Foreign planes entering Canada were not challenged. I wanted to confide in someone but kept silent. If I spoke with T.J., he might tell Mother and she, on medication for high blood pressure, would worry. Was Edmonton defended at all?

The Grade Eight term started and Sister Edwin did nothing to calm my fears.

"Very soon," she stated, lowering her head as if to pray," the Americans will resort to atomic weapons. The Russians will retaliate. World War Three. Canada is doomed."

Sister Edwin, I thought, should have known better. The Soviet army wasn't in Korea. But students never contradicted our school principal. Instead, under the guise of a Social Studies assignment, I drew a Korean map on the side blackboard and hoped she would have a new insight. I used blue chalk for the sea, red for the large communist-controlled area, yellow as the battle line, orange for city names and, running out of color choices, green over the U.N.'s small square at Pusan.

The map, I mused, resembled a distorted traffic light seen against the sky.

Each week the green square became smaller. Abruptly, as if he were part Irish, General MacArthur aimed at Seoul's orange target half-way up the map; his troops landed at Inchon and charged inland. North Korean forces retreated in disarray. My map's green expanded upward and the communist zone became a thin strip on the Yalu River. The war was almost won—without, I was relieved to note, Russian involvement.

Then China announced "volunteers" were going to Korea. The red tide again flooded south—General MacArthur, newscasters said, had asked President Truman's permission to use A-bombs on China's industrial base in Manchuria.

Our class was marched off to confession.

6   IT'S ONLY MAKE BELIEVE

The day-to-day terror was omnipresent. We were here this moment; we could be vapors in the next. Yearly, polio epidemics trained us to breathe shallowly; the nuclear threat taught us to breathe quietly. In church, school and home, acceptable behavior was drum-beat into our brains: confess your sins, stay in line and obey, obey the rules. We—the first generation in the atomic age—felt it, I think, the most. It. The pervasive pressure. The feeling that air, heavy as water, impeded our every movement. The feeling of being shuffled along in deathly slow motion. The feeling of being crushed down like a spring—and of wanting to explode.

Sister Edwin increased the torque on our teen-age psyches. "On graduation from Grade Eight," she intoned, "you will be transferred to Grandin School and into the hands of the Faithful Companions of Jesus. Their order, you will find, is more strict than my own Sisters of Halifax."

The F.C.J.'s were a fearsome lot but Grandin had, in its auxiliary teachers, a distinct polarity: Mr. McNamara was a world removed from Miss Bruce.

McNamara was what would now be called a hawk. When Harry Truman recalled Douglas MacArthur to Washington and relieved him of his command, our male teacher was livid. "A perfect example of how politicians bugger, excuse me girls, the whole world. Truman should have let the air force bomb those Commies into dust."

Miss Bruce—and I have often wondered how many there were like her speaking across North America to classes like ours—put it differently.

"If they didn't use the A-bomb in Korea, *then they'll never use it ever.*"

I looked across the room. Red's eyes had widened. He looked at me, gave a relieved grin and blinked twice. Our gang's secret sign of sudden enlightenment. Red knew. I knew. We were going to live.

And that evening, spinning the radio dial, I found Steve Woodman.

7   LEARNING THE GAME

"...so the four of us were standing at the bus stop when this guy with earphones runs out yelling 'CKUA's announcers all phoned in sick and the newscaster's fainted; get in here and help.' Guess we're supposed to play these records. What'll it be Pappy?"

"Booze!" The raucous voice cackled. "If they don't got any in this artsy-fartsy sweat-shop, at least play me a good drinking song."

"Martha," Steve asked, "what would you like to hear?"

"Really, Steven," came the pearl-toned, falsetto reply, "I wonder how I've tolerated this man for fifty years. He's a layabout. My friends pity me. I'm thankful none of them listens to this station."

"Friends?" Pappy exploded. "Those old hens? They buy a radio, plug it in and listen to static. I've offered to go over and twist their knobs but so far nobody's accepted."

"I think," Martha replied, "you could do with some inspirational music. Steven, play a song extolling the work ethic or," she sighed, "any ethic."

"Right," said Steve. "Drinking song. Work song. Teeny, what would tickle your little ears?"

"I dunno, Uncle Stevie," a very young child squeaked. "Maybe a nursery rhyme."

Steve played a triple: Spike Jones' *Cocktails For Two*, complete with cowbells, whistles, gulps and burps; George Formby's *When I'm Cleaning Windows*, with its bawdy overtones; and the absolutely rowdy, pulpit-thumping *Little Bo Beep/Grandma's Lyesoap*; the latter had been banned by many radio stations after preachers protested the parody. I instantly liked CKUA.

The program continued. Midnight approached. I was drowsily happy when Teeny snapped my eyelids open.

"Uncle Stevie," she inquired, "how come there's so many love songs on the radio? Why don't they play music for us kids?"

"Well," answered Steve, "when you're older you'll realize that little kids follow love songs—after about nine months. Takes that long 'cause you have to grow a bit. How old are you?"

"Five."

"Born in 1946. So, to sign off, I'll play a record for your mom and dad. Here's Glenn Miller's *In the Mood*."

I lay awake. Restless. Friday night. I had been listening to the radio. At home. Alone. I should have been dating. Grade Nine—and I was still single. Miss Bruce had said we'd all survive.That meant I'd end up being married some day. The search for a mate had to start Monday. Anytime after might be too late—all the pretty girls would be engaged before Christmas. And I did not want to be stuck with Frances.

"Sorry," Annette shrugged, "my cousin's visiting from Montreal this weekend."

Marie's relatives were also gathering, from Quebec City.

I reasoned the French girls' family ties made them permanently unavailable. Pauline said she had to study. Patsy thought she was getting chicken-pox. Frances sat across the aisle. I leaned over.

"Doing anything this weekend?"

"Yes," she spat. "I'm knitting little boy voodoo dolls. There's one in my desk." She opened the drawer. "This ruler is aimed at its head."

The ruler dropped. A stinging blow snapped my head around. "Sit up straight," ordered Mother Igneous, massaging her red palm as the noon bell, and my ears, rang.

Ape was incredulous, but not about the voodoo doll. "You tried to date Frances?"

"Naw," I countered. "But she makes the other turn-downs seem better."

Richard sauntered over with the smug air of an elder statesman. "You guys have trouble getting dates? It's easy in my room. Two girls for every boy. I'm taking out the sexiest girl in the class on Friday. Maybe she has a friend. Want me to set you up?"

I declined. Blind dates could be disasters. But maybe...

After school I waited at the bicycle rack. Jenny floated down the stairs. She had to be Richard's girl friend. I fumbled with the bike lock. She approached. Her long gold hair bounced unnaturally off her tightly-sweatered chest. My mouth dried. She spoke.

"Hi."

"Hello. Going anywhere special on Friday?"

"No." She looked puzzled.

"Richard taking you to a movie?"

"Nope. I'm free Friday."

"Like to see a show?"

"Sure. Pick me up at eight."

Ecstasy. I had lucked out. She rode off, not noticing my pant cuff had tangled in my bike chain.

Preparation time. What to wear. What to say. Memorize list of topics in case the movie had a long line-up. Money from the bank account. Bus tickets. Haircut. Shampoo. Major choice: Wildroot or Brylcream for the hair; settle on Brylcream because Wildroot's perfume too strong for indoors. Day arrives. School blurs. Home for a bath. Get dressed and shine shoes. Wash polish off hands. Check old papers for movie reviews. Wash newsprint off fingers. Final check in mirror. One hair standing straight up is carefully scissored away. Ready. Sit on chesterfield. Six o'clock. Two hours to go. The evening planned—like a military manoeuvre. Telephone rings. I answer. It's Jenny. Stomach sinks.

"About tonight..."

"Yeah?"

"How'd you like to bring some records over. We'll play them after the show."

Joy again. Choose records. Dust each one. Scotch-tape tears in paper jackets. Wash hands. Straighten tie. Walk to her house. Stop at hedge to wipe dust off shoes with pant leg. Brush pants. Take deep breath. Turn onto her sidewalk. Bump into Richard coming out.

"You too?" he said. "We've been had. Her little sister said she took off with some high school guys an hour ago. Jenny's had this party lined up for a month. Her sister said she skipped school this afternoon to have her hair done. She even bought a new dress last week, the bitch."

We stood outside the tall hedge until a quarter past eight.

"She's not coming back," I snarled. "Bitch. Let's go shoot some pool."

We wandered downtown. The sign over the dirty doorway said, "NO MINORS." We entered, went downstairs and paused at the elevated desk. A very fat man, wearing a green visor and chewing on an unlit cigar snapped his newspaper.

"How old are you?" He didn't look at us.

We added our ages and gave the standard reply. "We're twenty-eight."

"Hide in the can if the cops show up." He waved us on.

"Hey you guys, over here." Robert's voice. My eyes accustomed to the dark. Red was with him.

"My, my," Red admired, "don't we look pretty tonight."

"Just trying to bring a little class to this joint," Richard grunted.

"Records, too," Robert gushed. "Music while we play. How nice."

I picked up a pool cue. "How'd you like an extra belly-button?"

Billiard balls clicked, ran and dropped. We settled into the game. I calmed down; Robert sensed the change. He sidled over, chalking his cue.

"I assume you've been stood up."

"Yeah."

"Grade Niner?" He would not inquire further; it was insensitive to pry.

"Yeah."

"My sister told me not to bother dating. She said when she was in Grade Nine the girls battled each other to go out with high-schoolers. You were a failure if you went with somebody your own age."

"Who're we supposed to date then?"

"Whore?"

"You know what I mean. We can't compete with Grade Tens and we won't take out those babies in Grade Eight. Who's left?"

"Nobody," Robert said, lining up his shot. "We're on hold." He smashed the white ball ahead. "For an entire, lonely year."

Hours passed. We stood at the bus stop. T.J. was driving home from his club and gave us a lift. He and I entered the house.

"Date go sour?"

I nodded. He listened and, unexpectedly, laughed. "She's a trophy hunter! There's only one way to deal with them. You're sure the little sister didn't see you?"

I phoned Jenny the next morning and apologized profusely for having gone to play pool. I'd not noticed the time slipping by until midnight when, of course, it was too late to call. Perhaps we'd see each other at school. Yes? I'd get in touch some time.

I never got around to speaking to her again. As T.J. said, "After a few years all the boys'll catch on and she'll be smelling her armpits, wondering what happened."

8 SIXTEEN TONS

Libidos in limbo, we concentrated our energy on studying for the province-wide Departmental Examinations. Because the Social Credit government's power base was in rural Alberta, we city kids had to memorize types of cattle, varieties of grain, compositions of topsoil and lists of cabinet ministers' names. "Politicians," Mr. McNamara told us, "try to give their voters' kids an edge." He was right: even math problems were described in gallons of milk and bushels of wheat.

The exams' rustic orientation reminded me: scout camp was imminent. Since a nuclear war was not coming and survival training therefore unnecessary, I saw no logical reason to abandon the amenities of civilization for two weeks. I balked.

"Major Campbell has my cheque," Mother stated firmly. "You're going."

The scout camp on Pigeon Lake, sixty miles south of Edmonton, was separated from the water by a rocky southern shoreline. I had spent summers at Ma-Me-O's sandy beach on the lake's eastern side and had taken the water expanse for granted: lakes just happened—they were there. Mr. McNamara, in one of his intense study sessions, posed a question. "Why," he asked, "are there so many lakes on the prairies that water flows in to but never out of?" He cited Pigeon. "Streams pour toward it and rain falls on it, but the only outflow is a pitiful little creek that would keep a family of mice thirsty." He let us mull the matter for three days. Our minds failed to guess the mysterious solution. "Alberta's lakes," he declared, "drain into a vast underground river system that spans the prairies. The province is sitting on porous sedimentary rock formed as the primeval ocean receded. Where the jungles were, there's now coal, oil and gas; and the old riverbeds are hidden today a mile beneath the ground." We thought he was daft.

I retained the information in case a question arose on the Departmentals. At scout camp I tried to salvage my wasted time by being a hero. If Mr. McNamara was correct, there would certainly be a whirlpool at the centre of Pigeon Lake; Major Campbell should be alerted to the danger.

"Balderdash!" he humphed. His close-cropped military mustache gave a superior quiver. "The lake's not a bathtub nor," he peered at me closely, "the home of the Loch Ness Monster—if that's what your imagination is going to conjure up next. Clear the ground, pitch your tent and be ready for parade in an hour."

I rejoined the Cougar patrol. Red was dissecting a twig with his buffalo-skinner's knife. Ape sat nearby with sunlight falling on the Neanderthal brow, casting deep shadows over his orbits. Robert, short and thin, stood on tiptoes following a caterpillar's progress up a poplar tree. Richard skipped stones across the water. Mert, physical as usual, counted his fortieth push-up.

"Okay, guys," Mert shouted. "Time to make camp." He had, since Grade Eight, been a mainstay of the St. Joseph's *High School* basketball team. Through athletic dedication—rather than academic effort—Mert flunked Grade Nine and was a year older than we, still at Grandin, and the natural selection as patrol leader.

Our campsite was on a small flatland between the lake and a short hill leading to an abandoned farm field. On the far side of the field was the outhouse; west sat the leader's quarters—a shack—and beyond it our fieldstone and log camp kitchen. Mert surveyed the hill.

"I think the guys last year pitched their tent here." He pointed to a weed-infested clearing in the trees.

It is extraordinary how quickly prairie grasses fill nature's vacuums—and how tenaciously they grip the earth. We had the site partially cleared when a bugle sounded.

"Damn," Red exclaimed, "if he keeps us on parade half an hour the weeds'll grow back."

The troop formed a circle by the kitchen. Major Campbell stood on the doorway's cement step. He cleared his throat.

"Again, this year, we are honored to have Miss Swenson as camp cook."

Groans issued from thirty famished faces. Her reputation had preceded her. Robert's francophone description of Miss Swenson's roast chicken was "dead bird *avec* feathers *flambeau*." Ape graphically depicted her fish casserole as "scales, skin, bones and guts, with eyeballs as a bonus in your bowl." Richard said, regarding the wizened, spinster sister of a district farmer, "When she starts to look like your ideal date, you've been at camp too long."

"Order!" barked the Major. He leaned to his left as Miss Swenson grasped his sleeve. He shook his head. Miss Swenson smiled and departed. Major Campbell was incredulous as he watched her become even smaller in the distance. "She wanted a raise. I refused. She quit." We cheered. The Major tugged his belt up over the ample belly. "Alright you varlets." His smile was a strange combination of benign paternalism and malignant foreboding. "You feed yourselves for a fortnight." He looked directly at me and Mert. "The Cougar Patrol will bestow their culinary favors upon us." Everybody, except the Cougars, cheered.

Mert's voice echoed in the huge cast-iron stove. "I'll start the fire and," he added magnanimously, "you guys cook the meal."

Richard paled. Robert developed a tremor. Ape excused himself and went to the outhouse. I shuffled.

"Well, second-in-command," Red grinned at me, "looks like you're the chef for today. Don't worry. Richard and I'll round up dessert. How's saskatoon pie sound?"

"Okay. I guess."

"No, dummy," Red admonished. "It sounds bubble-bubble, yum-yum. We'll be back in a wink."

While Mert busied himself with the fire, I cut and stir-fried cubed beef inches. Robert peeled, sliced and boiled potatoes and carrots. I wiped his knife and, as I had seen Mother do, held it in my teeth. As Mother had predicted, irritating onion vapors did not reach my eyes; cold steel was an effective barrier against tears. I added water to the beef pan and fried the onions. When Ape returned, I started him kneading dough with a debarked log as his rolling pin. I poured vegetable water into the frying pan, scraped its encrustations with a fork, then added flour to make brown gravy. I tossed the meat, vegetables and gravy together to simmer. Red and Richard appeared with a back-pack full of berries. We dumped the load into a bucket of water, picked worms off the surface and layered the fruit on Ape's pastry shells. A line was forming outdoors. "We want food!" it shouted. To placate the mob, I threw a handful of salt on the stew and a handful of sugar on each pie. We opened the doors.

Major Campbell approached the amorphous mass on his tin plate with trepidation. His eyebrows lifted as a beef cube split cleanly on the touch of his fork. He tasted. He ate. He cleaned his tray.

"Who," the Major burped, "concocted this meal?" Five fingers pointed at me. "And is it too much to expect dessert?"

Ape snapped to attention and I sliced the freshly-baked saskatoon pies. The Major took a bite.

"Who, may I again ask, is responsible for this?"

I experienced a queasiness as five fingers again aimed at me. I felt my cheeks blushing.

The Major fumbled in his pocket and extracted a felt circle. "Usually I award the Camp Cook badge on our final night. However," he continued, "I can't imagine a better meal." He handed me the trophy and raised his voice. "The Cougar Patrol is relieved of further K.P. duties after tomorrow morning." We Cougars cheered—alone.

Robert, anxious to do something after peeling the vegetables, had taken a can-opener to a dozen tins of clams.

"They look like dinks," Richard observed keenly. "What'll we do? They'll be rotten tomorrow."

"Simple," I assured him with new-found confidence. "Just leave them in water overnight."

The next morning I served the troop clam omelettes. Yellow egg yolk-color combined quite well, I thought, with green clam guts. The Major forced down one bite.

"Stick to stew," he snarled.

The Coyotes burned lunch and the Beavers scorched supper. The Wolf Patrol's morning porridge glued the Major's spoon and bowl together.

"Attention," he roared. We were silent. He looked hungry. "In Normandy, under constant barrage, I did not miss a meal." He swallowed heavily. His voice was plaintive. "Yet in peacetime, when all should be neatly-ordered, I have been without food FOR TWENTY-FOUR HOURS!"

His gaze swept around the circle and paused at the Cougar Patrol. I knew what he was thinking. His eyelids smiled as he recalled the stew, startled into omelette-shape when he remembered breakfast and became threatening slits while he issued the ultimatum.

"Rations will be apportioned each patrol at their campsites. You shall eat what you cook. Avoid starving; cannibalism has been known to occur in similar situations."

Robert beside me looked like a frightened rabbit. Stewed rabbit. My stomach gurgled. Robert jumped.

The Major reached a trembling hand downward and poured a cup of coffee. "Thank God," he said, "nobody can ruin this." He drank, spat and glowered.

"But sir," the Wolf leader protested, "I kept it boiling since sunrise."

Under Mert's direction we dug three pits: one lined with flat rocks, for the fire; a second, near lakeside, as a cooler; and the third—as close as possible to the Wolves—for garbage.

Mert called us together. "The Major gave me one match."

Red stepped forward. "My Indian forefathers passed on to me the secret of making fire. First, you gather together tiny splinters and dry bark. Then you make a pile of bigger twigs. Then you get small logs and finally..."

"You light the match," Robert piped.

"No, dummy," Red grimaced, rummaging an arm into his sleeping bag, "you put it all on...this newspaper. My grandpa says it beats birchbark all to hell."

The fire blazed. Ape tucked a last beef patty into the cast-iron pan and approached the grill. Red's hand rested paternally on Ape's forearm.

"Not so fast. My forefathers say a frying pan is like a woman—get'em both hot before the meat goes in."

"What's that mean?" Robert whispered.

"I dunno," I replied, "but it sounds good."

Red let the orange and yellow flames dwindle to scarlet embers. He flicked drops of water on the pan and nodded as they danced and disappeared.

"Hamburger time," he announced.

The Major arrived on tour. Evidently pleased, he walked away a few paces, paused, and pointed a thumb over his shoulder.

"The Wolves are having trouble," he said. "Send them a flaming faggot."

We looked silently at each other.

"I think he means the wood," Mert said, backing away.

Richard's eyes darted around his cluster of tent-mates. "I *hope* he means the wood."

Night came. Red and I, neither sleepy, sat stoking the fire. Someone inside our tent had blown out the kerosene lantern and we heard snoring.

"Roll call," Ape shouted in the blackness.

"Shee-it," Richard swore.

"How'd you like a frigging sock in your throat," Mert cursed.

"Present," Robert mumbled.

Richard crawled through the tent flap and rubbed his hands above the flickering coals.

Red's voice was casual. "What'd you say in there?" He was up to something—again.

"I said," Richard answered, "shee-it."

The ebbing firelight flashed off Red's dark eyes. "Let's go looking."

Richard sat upright. "For *she*?"

"No, you Yankee numbskull, for *it*."

"What's *it*?" I asked.

"The light in the night," Red replied.

"You're a poet and you didn't know it".

"I make a rhyme every time. Come on. There's no moon tonight. This'll be easy."

We followed the shoreline away from camp. Red scrambled up a hill. "Nothing," he said, "yet." We staggered a further hundred yards among the rocks. Red swung on a branch and landed in a small clearing by the lake. I could see his arm extended toward the bush. "Bingo."

A ghostly glow bordered the meadow. Trees felled by long-extinguished fires shone a phosphorescent fungal green as if ancient lightning had been trapped on the forest floor. Fluttering moths gave the radiance a sense of motion. The trees were dead, but their wood was again alive. *It*—an unburning luminosity with mysterious power; a frozen fire we held in our hands. We did not speak while carrying the treasure back to camp. *It* was sacred.

We hid the glowing wood behind our tent and returned to the fire-pit's reddish warmth. Red leaned forward, blew a flame to life and watched it vanish.

"I think," he said, "the Wolves should experience a light in the night."

"Them?" Richard exclaimed. "You're kidding."

"Nope," Red chuckled, "those guys need something to brighten them up. Get a shovel."

Guided by the Wolves' kerosene lantern, we entered their camp and moved the woodpile off its rubberized groundsheet. Red shoveled a knee-deep pit at the tent entrance while Richard patted the diggings into a berm around the hole. Red lined the trap with the groundsheet. I filled the pool with lakewater. We laid logs atop the berm crest and bridged them with bark chips. Red emptied the lantern's reservoir generously along the wood.

"Okay you guys, gather up some rocks and hide in the bush. When I signal, chuck and yell like crazy."

Red lifted the lantern's globe. After Richard and I were in position, he swept the flame along the logs. A spectacular blaze erupted.

The Wolves—including one still adorned with his sleeping bag—stood in water watching the last wisp of flame lift harmlessly off the earthen barrier. Their leader, marginally smarter than the rest, summed up the soggy saga.

"I think," he said, "somebody tricked us."

We retired to our tent. Richard could not stop giggling.

"Get some sleep," Red cautioned. "They'll be after us at sunrise."

"Not likely," Richard gasped.

"How come?"

"I smeared their tent front with marmalade."

The Wolves were late when reveille sounded. Very late. The Major investigated, strolled into our camp and tried not to smile.

"It seems the Wolves failed to post a sentry last night." He looked at Mert. "Nice touch, that."

"What, sir?" Mert asked, appropriately befuddled.

"The jam. Stroke of genius. The place is swarming with wasps and ants. The Wolves are trapped: can't run or they'll get stung and can't crawl or they'll get bit." He awarded Mert the Stalker's Badge for "hunting and studying six wild animals in their natural state."

"What's going on?" Mert wondered as the Major departed.

"I dunno," said Richard, feigning innocence. "But if Ape cooks the bacon and eggs, and Robert doesn't burn the toast, Red, Billy and I'll do the dishes."

Richard's prescience was uncanny. The three of us were busily scrubbing at lakeside when the Wolves came calling. Mert met them and denied everything.

"Scout's honor?" demanded their leader.

Mert held up the two-finger salute. "Scout's honor. None of us left camp last night."

"How about them?" The revenge-seeker pointed toward the lake.

"Not a chance," replied Mert. "They sleep at the back and I'd of heard them if they got up."

That night a de-pegged tent collapsed on the guiltless Beavers. We suspected the Wolves were responsible but Richard doubted they had the ingenuity.

Red awakened us with the aroma of freshly-caught pickerel sizzling in butter. The Wolves came begging.

"Catch your own," Red remarked casually. He tossed them his hook and line. The Wolves scurried to the rowboat and paddled far out on the lake. We were finishing our meal when Red's head snapped up. "Let's go to the pier and watch."

We saw oars hit the water and, after several seconds, heard the sound. A Wolf teetered, cupped his hands and sat. "Quiet!"

We eavesdropped. The boat drifted closer to shore.

Mert was impatient. "Come on guys. We got work to do."

"Wait," Red muttered, looking at the sky. "They got a chance at jack."

Mert stood. "Let's go."

"There!" Red shouted.

The rowboat erupted. A jackfish flashed across the stern. Several hands pulled on the line. The fish resisted. Water splashed. A Wolf struck with his hatchet.

"I thought so," remarked Red.

We watched, thoroughly entertained, as the boat began sinking. Two Wolves paddled. Three bailed. One waved a frantic semaphore.

"What's he signalling?" Robert asked.

Ape gazed seaward. "U-R-N," he replied.

"They need a bucket," Red purred.

Major Campbell surveyed the shipwreck and addressed his troop assembled on the beach. We gained, as he spoke, an even greater respect for the man.

"In battle, generals try to win regardless of cost. It is the lesser officers' job to conduct the campaign with a minimum loss of life. Generals decide when and where to fight; we determine *how*. Scout Rules recommend an overnight canoe campout for each patrol but I will not allow a group showing suicidal tendencies," he looked at the Wolves, "near water more than waist deep. Therefore, while others are away, the Wolves will gather rocks and extend the pier so fishing can be done despite our defunct rowboat." Muffled applause was cut off by the Major's right arm sweeping downward. "The campout is scheduled three days hence. All patrols will help the Wolves until then, but only the two most industrious will be allowed to make the trip. Construction starts thirteen-thirty hours. Dismissed."

Richard was angry. "It's not fair."

"We pay to work," added Red, sharing the disgruntlement.

"There's no way," Ape stated, "I'm gonna leave this tent and sleep under spruce boughs. You guys can build the pier. I'll watch."

"Where's the canoe trip go?" I asked.

Mert seemed amused. "Fisher Home. It's a little post office and general store. You can buy candy and comics there."

"Big deal," grumbled Richard.

"There's sand on the beach."

"Hoo-ray."

"And it's right next to the girls' camp."

"The wieners and beans are cooked," Robert announced.

We gulped lunch and rocketed into action. Robert and I loaded stones onto stretchers fashioned from groundsheets and staves. Mert and Richard *ran* each load to the pier. Ape and Red wedged the rocks in place. Our only competition came from the Coyotes, who had formed a fairly efficient bucket brigade—and were working with unusual fervor.

"Dig faster," Mert ordered. "The Coyotes know about the girls."

We had stripped the beach and were extracting rocks from the lake bed.

"Is this worth it?" Robert asked.

"Yeah," I assured him. "*Females. Women.* They might even wave and talk to us as we paddle by."

We underestimated the girls.

The oldest Coyote, designated by the Major as an assistant scoutmaster, led our expedition. Kevin wore eight of the nine King's Scout badges on his left sleeve. Only the Horseman's Badge eluded him because he didn't have "a horse at his disposal".

We were packing our gear into the canoes when Mert paused to look at the Wolf-Beaver chain gang on the pier. "I feel kind of sorry for those guys moving tons of rock and all."

"Don't," Kevin replied. "The Major knows what he's doing. He'll be taking them out himself next week. You guys know how to survive—he claims—so you get the honor of camping with the old, experienced Coyotes."

"Learned how to cook yet?" Mert asked. "Your grilled cheese sandwiches..."

"Point made," Kevin cut him off. The Coyotes had buttered the bread *inside* and literally flamed the sandwiches over an open fire. "We're having hot-dogs tonight. Can't go wrong."

"Plain old hot-dogs?" Mert inquired.

"Yeah," Kevin smirked. "Think you can handle it? You need sticks. Don't use your fingers."

"We use toothpicks."

"Huh?"

Mert called to Robert. "Tell this barbarian about hot-dogs."

Robert lowered his knapsack. "You slit the wieners lengthwise, fill them with cheese, wrap a strip of bacon along and hold it all together with toothpicks." He pointed to us. We chanted.

"The frying pan cooks the bacon and the bacon broils the weenie and the weenie melts the cheese..." We looked at Mert.

"...and the Cougars dine in the wilderness," Mert concluded. He couldn't resist twisting the dagger. "They're 'specially good if the buns are *just so* lightly toasted."

Canoes terrified Ape. Heights didn't bother him—he climbed trees that daunted the rest of us. On the ground, he was a fierce competitor in football: three opponents was the minimum necessary for a tackle. His phobia was smothering in water.

"Grab the canoe sides," Mert reassured him. "Step onto the middle beam. Keep your balance, then sit down. Stay in the centre and don't lean. Billy and I'll do the paddling. Nothing to it."

We stroked westward away from the pier: five times at the right front with a simultaneous five at the back, then switch. Within minutes the camp disappeared behind a small headland.

"Look ahead and north," Mert instructed. "Just check south to get your bearings. Sunlight on the water can give you snow-blindness." He considered Ape's uneasiness. "You're our navigator. Keep us near the shore, but not so close we'll hit a sandbank."

A breeze brushed our foreheads. Waves appeared on the water. Mert and I both paddled port to enter the waves and starboard to ride them. The passage was smooth. Ape relaxed. A voice far behind interrupted our concentration.

"Hey," Kevin yelled. "Tighten up this convoy. Major's orders."

Mert peered ahead. "I think I can see the girls' cabins. We'll slow down there and let the rest catch up. That'll give us a longer look."

"I ain't lookin'," Ape declared. "I don't wanna go blind."

"Nuts," said Mert. "There's a few clouds now. The glare off the water won't be so bad."

"Not now," Ape muttered. "Tonight when we bed down and think about seeing them."

I recalled the schoolyard warning and laughed. "No way. Playing with yourself doesn't cause blindness; it just grows hair on your hands." I glanced back. Mert was checking his palms. "Gotcha," I said.

"Go comb your fingers," Mert countered.

Ape's hands stayed clutched on the canoe's railings; either he wasn't fooled or he didn't fool around.

Ahead, I saw two tiny figures on the beach. They saw us and scurried away.

"They're hiding," I said to Ape. "Relax."

"Wait," Mert cautioned. "They'll be back."

The canoe bow swung north as I, fascinated by the scene on the shore, forgot to change sides while stroking. Girls poured from their cabins and materialized out of the bush. They bounced, huddled, shucked clothing and plunged into the water.

"Paddle on starboard." I didn't need Mert's order and had already aimed our canoe toward the dozen bobbing heads. I looked at the beach: larger figures were restraining stragglers. "Paddles up," Mert instructed. I watched water drip off the oar and rested it on the canoe's bow. We drifted.

The heads grew larger; we saw yellow, red and black hair. An arm rose above the water.

"Hi," the nearest blonde greeted us. She had obviously dog-paddled out: her curls were undisturbed.

I was confused. "Hello."

Mert was confident. "Hi yourself, you lovely little mermaid."

"And lead us not into temptation." Ape's face directed the prayer northward.

A brunette rolled in the water and surfaced. "Some of us aren't wearing bathing suits," she said. "See if you can guess who." With that command, the entire group duck-dived and flashed buttocks, legs and feet. I cursed the sunlight: each temptress had a twin.

The blonde took charge. "Kick your feet and wave your arms!" The bodies lept out of the water.

"They got boobs?" Mert asked.

"Bubbles," I answered. "Just bubbles."

A whistle sounded then, urgently, tweeted again. The girls swam toward shore.

Kevin's boat drew abreast; the others followed. Our flotilla blocked the cove.

"See anything?" Kevin sounded jealous.

"Only water," Ape stated, affirming his purity.

Mert became our spokesman. "I saw some bums but it was hard..."

Kevin interrupted. "I can believe it."

Richard had the final word. "Girls that skinny-dip," he said, "never wear pyjamas. Let's visit their camp tonight."

We landed at Fisher Home, constructed lean-to shelters and dug a communal fire pit. We were restless.

"Let's visit the store," Ape suggested. We acceded: the post office was a logical first stop—most girls liked candy.

We followed a path to the store's front steps. Lounging on the wood veranda were two elderly women—they appeared to be about thirty years old. We passed unchallenged, made our purchases and milled around outside. The taller woman spoke. She had wispy dark hair on her upper lip.

"Camping?"

"Yep," Kevin replied.

"So are we." She unsheathed a huge knife. "We'd like to meet any girls in your party."

"We don't got girls with us," Kevin answered.

"That," said the woman, slicing the knife above her left fist, "can be arranged."

Our enthusiasm shrivelled and we shrank back to camp. Supper was silent. Mert had scoured our frying pan and while drying the spatula, paused. "She's bluffing. Who's ready for a midnight hunting party?"

"Not me," said Richard. "You get a gander at her muscles? I've got a feeling *she* was once a *he*. You want to be called 'Myrtle' the rest of your life?"

Mert opened his mouth but Red silenced him. "Listen."

The breeze had become a wind. Cloud covered the sky. Red's finger pointed at the trees. Distant single, then staccato tapping resounded from the forest. Rain, heard before it was felt, cooled our ardor and gave us an honorable excuse to remain celibate overnight.

Kevin's Coyotes—to his credit—had taken shifts and kept the fire alive. We breakfasted on fried corned beef mixed into rubbery eggs. The sky was blue, but there were whitecaps on the water.

"Maybe we should portage the canoes," Richard suggested.

"Yeah," Red perked, "along the shore past the girls' camp."

Kevin squelched the idea. "Ixnay. The Major sent me out with Tenderfoot Scouts; I'm not goin' back with Tendercrotch Guides."

We had roused at first light and, after watching a spectacular orange and violet sunrise, loaded the canoes. We howled while passing the girls' camp but the place looked deserted. Red's canoe pulled alongside.

"Bet they're scratching at the windows," he said.

Robert appeared disconsolate. "What's it matter? We're not going to meet them."

"Yeah," Richard sounded disheartened. "I'm sure there's a plot to keep us away from girls. It'll be no better in high school: camp counsellors are just F.C.J.'s in mufti."

"They want us to be priests." Robert's voice was barely audible.

"Right!" Mert's paddle smacked the water. "Let's practice. Robert'll hear Red's confession and Ape'll hear mine."

I swivelled. Ape's hands were cupped over his ears. I gazed at the other canoe. Robert's head was bowed; Richard seemed on the verge of tears.

Our canoes surged ahead, avoiding a bullrush-packed peninsula, and glided across a barely submerged field of seaweed. The sound on the canoe's keel was familiar. I looked up. Major Campbell stood on an elongated pier. Wolves and Beavers, sleeping bags and knapsacks, cluttered the rocky headland. The Major greeted Kevin.

"Changed my plans. The weather bureau says we're in the eye of a storm front. One calm day out and back before we get socked in for the duration. Here," he tossed Kevin a shiny, jingling cluster, "take my car keys. If you need anything, get it at the Westerose store."

The Major barked like a coxswain and the re-manned canoes skimmed away with, I mused, incredible efficiency. We retired to camp, dropped our kits and headed for the kitchen.

"Peanut butter," Red moaned. "My body needs peanut butter."

I slammed the last cupboard door. "Nothing except flour and sugar. Those crafty bastards wanna starve us."

"No bread?" Mert asked.

"One slice," I answered, "but it's turning blue."

"Peanut butter, " Red rasped. He extracted a crumpled dollar bill from his pocket. "I'll pay."

The Coyotes arrived. We pooled resources and composed a shopping list. Kevin looked at the money.

"One problem," he said. "None of us can drive."

"I can." Richard stepped forward. "Nothing to it. Gimme the keys."

Kevin hesitated. "You're not old enough to have a license."

Richard took a deep breath and pointed at Red. "Mercy mission. Anyway, the Mounties wouldn't bother to patrol the Westerose road."

Richard, Ape, Robert and I piled into Major Campbell's sun-roofed Austin. I had never been in a smaller car. Richard rolled down the window. Kevin's head poked through.

"Look you guys," he said, balancing with his hands while his feet slipped away, "it rained pretty heavy last night and there's mud everywhere. Be careful."

Richard seemed perturbed. "Key's in the ignition. Foot's on the clutch. Hand's on the choke. Other foot's on the gas. Bugger off."

We jack-rabbited out of the campground with lurching starts and thudding halts. The car's engine protested; the gear-box ground its teeth. We eventually bumped onto the main road. Richard wheeled right.

"Uh, Richard," I interrupted, "Westerose is left."

"I know," he snarled, "but the girls—and Fisher Home—are this way."

"Madness," Ape declared. "We're either gonna get killed from your driving or de-balled by that Amazon. Lunacy! 'Fess up. You ever driven before?"

"Just once. On my uncle's farm in Texas. He let me steer the tractor."

Ape was not consoled. "Steers are the cow equivalent of gelded horses. Turn back."

"Nuts," Richard replied.

"Exactly," Ape affirmed.

We flew down a hill and splashed into a puddle. Brown mud obscured the front windshield. Richard, unable to locate the wipers, opened the Austin's sunroof and stood on the driver's seat. "Ape," he commanded, "work the gas pedal. Robert, scrunch up here between my feet and push the brake when I tell you."

I, alone in the back seat, felt a sense of imminent doom as we hurtled forward: it would have been more sensible to stop and clean the window but Richard was undeterred as he directed our guided missile.

"More gas! Touch the brake and let go!" I saw him lean backward from wind resistance as we gathered speed. It was like a midway ride—without tracks. A rapid scan of my conscience indicated a recent confession would have been prudent. My stomach dropped as we sped down another hill. Muddy water cascaded by the side windows. We slammed to a stop in the centre of a slough.

"We skidded off the road," Richard said redundantly. He gunned the engine to no avail. "We're stuck. Not to worry. We'll flag a car and get a tow."

It was twilight before Richard decided he had taken a side road with no traffic. He doffed his shoes and socks, waded to an adjacent field, and trekked back in the direction of a farmhouse I recalled we had passed. He returned.

"Woman there says her husband'll be sober by morning and he'll pull us out with his tractor. Better bed down for the night Open the windows a crack. We'll need air."

I couldn't sleep. My hunger pangs were matched by those of mosquito hordes that found their way into the car. Each insect, I decided, was using my ears as a beacon in making its final approach to a landing site. Between slapping dozens of predators, I observed something I had hitherto not noticed: the moon moved. Up until that night I had considered the moon as stationary in the sky; when it finally sank in the west, the eastern sky had begun to glow. A tractor motor rumbled and I shook Richard's shoulder. He scratched his bare feet and slogged toward the farmer. Voices were raised.

"Five dollars? That's our grocery money."

"Five dollars," stated the farmer. "Pay up or stay there."

We abandoned the Fisher Home expedition and drove back to camp. Kevin was livid—but conciliatory.

"We sort of figured you fouled up," he said, "so we went begging."

Miss Swenson appeared at the kitchen door. "Breakfast's ready," she announced. It was delicious.

The remaining days passed quickly but one recurring thought nagged me: Grade Ten started in September. St. Joe's was going co-ed because St. Mary's downtown was closing. The girls were coming to *our* school. Would the F.C.J.'s be with them?

9 MR. SANDMAN

"*Repetitio mater studiorum.* Repetition is the mother of learning."
Father Daly paused and frowned. "At St. Joseph's you will learn how to
think. Thinking is not memorization and mimicry. A lioness trains her
cubs by follow-the-leader example. Horses on bread and milk routes
remember where to stop. Dogs can obey dozens of voice commands.
Parrots imitate spoken words. Animals react to what is happening, while
humans anticipate that which has not yet occurred. If you are given a dozen
identical tasks, the twelfth will be easier than the first—repetition has
made it so. And if you are efficient in any job, there will be created,
magically, *time to think.*"

He cocked his head. Distant hammering from the north wing melded with
whining saws in the west extension. "St. Joseph's High School's motto is
'*Palma non sine pulvere.*' Hands not without dust, in strict translation. It
means this: to achieve, you must first change something, as did
Michaelangelo when he transformed marble blocks into life-like statues.
Consider our new building. The bricks are made of clay gouged from the
earth; the walls inside were once trees. The world elsewhere changed to
house us and," he said, peering over his wire-framed glasses, "we, in turn,
will change you."

Like an epicure sniffing a fine cigar, Father Daly passed a chalk stick
slowly under his nose. "Let us begin. The shortest distance between two
points is a straight line."

Within minutes he began to repeat himself. Our minds free, most of us
daydreamed, others doodled and a few heads nodded off in sleep. I felt
indescribably restless.

"What'd he mean?" Robert asked.

Red pointed to a particulate sunbeam near the blackboard."*Repetitio
mater pulverorum.* I think I'm learning Latin. Maybe he's teaching two
subjects at once."

"Three," I corrected. "Robert's been practicing art."

"Actually, fellows, the number is four. Add philosophy."

I turned toward the British-accented voice and started. Bushy mustache.
Jacket and tie. A teacher in our midst?

"Hello," he said. "My name's Alfred. I'm Anglican. Seen any girls?"

"Not at St. Joe's until..." I gestured at Robert.

"...Christmas, my sister says. She's in St. Mary's. Grade Eleven.
Anglican?"

"Yes. My dear *pater*," Alfred bowed toward Red, "wanted me in an all-boy institution. Where do I purchase a school tie?"

Red snickered. "The teachers have a necktie party after exams."

"Good show. Daddy will be pleased."

"And you'll be taller," I added.

Richard edged over. "How long you been in Canada?"

"Approximately five years."

"I lost my Texas accent in five months."

"Find it, old man. It'll do wonders when the girls arrive."

"We need all the help we can get," Richard replied. "Three of our Grade Nine girls got married during the summer. Age fourteen."

This was news to me. I hoped justice had prevailed. "Jenny?"

"Naw," Richard answered. "She's too crafty. Carries her own supply of party balloons."

"Oh," Alfred interjected. "She keeps the boys distracted by blowing them up?"

Red smirked. "You got the general idea."

Father Daly's class was our only lecture that day. A blur of teachers entered, gave us book lists, and exited. One lingered: Frank Schneider, a layman.

"You guys," he said, leaning casually against the doorway, "come from all parts of Edmonton. These three years are gonna determine where you end up as adults. Skid row or the crescents—your choice. I'll show you how to beat the odds and get ahead out there; you know how, it's easy. You wanna listen, I'll help. Ignore me, you're on your own." He vanished.

We met Mert and Ape by the bike racks. Twenty-eight in our class and twenty-nine in theirs.

"You seen Father Mac yet?" Ape asked.

We shook our heads, hoping the principal had been transferred.

Mert smiled. "The guys on the basketball team say he sits waiting for a chance to dive-bomb the Grade Tens. In Major Campbell's words, 'Be Prepared.'"

Father Mac attacked after the first snowfall. I missed the action by arriving at the school moments after the bell. I had awakened at the usual time, found my winter sweater and was picking wood chips—souvenirs from the Grade Nine shop lathe—out of the wool when I realized I'd have to take the bus. After storing my bicycle in the garage, I skidded to 124th Street and watched the trolley depart. The driver ignored my waving. I later thanked him.

"We're for it," Richard said, dangling his coat. "Dedicate the morning prayers to our filthy little souls."

"What happened?"

"Snowball fight."

"That's all?"

"Not exactly."

Father Daly shuffled to the window and stood, silently, looking at us. The priest folded his arms and half-turned to face the doorway; we knew what was imminent. My nose became itchy but I dared not move. Richard had the same contagious problem and raised his arm. Snap! Father Daly's fingers sent Richard's hand thudding onto the desktop. The back of my head became itchy; I didn't bother to scratch: my butterfly was settling in again. Similar situation. Sunlight through the windowbeams shadowed a cross on the blackboard. Church? The butterfly became agitated. Not church? It quieted. Our situation was similar to death-row in a federal institution—complete with a priest for last rites. Prison? The butterfly left, and the warden appeared.

Father MacDonald slammed the door and strode up and down five rows of frightened felons. I saw on his right wrist a leather thong and, attached to it, the riding-crop he used as a blackboard pointer. He patted the whip on his left hand while pacing. He towered; we cowered. Sparse grey hair; sharp, almost granite, facial rigidity; no lips; eyes like a hawk circling over field mice. He faced us, his tongue flicking out anticipating a feast. I expected guttural thunder. When a twang several octaves above tenor said, "So, the Grade Ten class has proven its manliness," I didn't know whether to laugh and die or stifle and suffocate. My butterfly began to alight but I mentally shooed it away—the high-pitched voice came straight from the Strand Theatre where, in a Saturday afternoon movie, the Gestapo commandant greeted his new prisoners. The whip smacked on the wall and resumed its gentle tapping. Next, I thought, he'll offer us a cigarette. Father Mac's hand went to his coat pocket. He extracted a copper coin.

"Here," he crooned, "is a penny for your thoughts. Who'll confess first?"

The class pretended stolidity.

"Come now," coaxed Father Mac as he licked saliva from his oral angles, "let me hear it from the bravest among you."

A chair scraped behind me. I didn't have to look. Alfred was standing. I doubted his sanity.

"Bless me, Father for I have sinned. I confess to Almighty God and to you, Father, that I directed a medieval arrow-shower against the infidel."

I had no idea what Alfred was owning up to but his letter-perfect recitation of the pre-confession prayer reassured me: the Anglican had done his homework and was tackling our common enemy on his home turf.

"Infidel?" Father MacDonald appeared confused.

"Yessir. He called us cat-lickers. As a Protestant, I felt my honor impugned."

Father Mac seemed fascinated. "Arrow shower?"

"Snowballs, actually. Appropriate punishment, sir, considering the provocation."

"I saw the entire incident from my office window. Please," he said with unexpected deference, "allow me to summarize my observation."

"Permission granted," Alfred replied—with foolhardy nonchalance. I concluded he was suicidal.

Father Mac's teeth bared: he sensed an easy kill. His upper-alto voice seethed with sarcasm. "A pre-school toddler—scarcely out of diapers—shouts at you, fashions a pitiful snowball and throws it spastically in your general direction. The harmless missile plumps on the road nearer him than you. In an instant, the poor little half-mitt is cascaded. He runs to the door and summons his mother."

"Regrettable, sir," Alfred interrupted. "She ran out while some snowballs were still in flight."

"Nonsense! You were like sharks in a feeding frenzy. The volley continued. Both of them were coated."

Alfred was undeterred. "And so they should have been. The child obviously learned religious prejudice from his parents. I only regret his father wasn't there."

Father Mac became nonplussed. He looked at Father Daly but saw his compatriot's eyes gazing neutrally skyward. "No recess breaks until Christmas," he muttered. "I'm tightening the screws for you lot."

Frank Schneider seemed amused. "Look on the positive side. The kid learned a lesson. What the hell," he said gathering his science notes with athletic dexterity. "You probably saved the little bugger's life."

Father Kelly drew a different perspective—our Social Studies teacher was reminded of the Korean War. "Little North Korea, by encroaching on other territory, brought upon itself the United Nation's combined wrath. Fortunately," he remarked, the purple vein on his forehead growing larger, "you were dissuaded from more drastic action. I am sure," he said, halting behind Alfred, "General MacArthur here would not have been content until he bombed the house into oblivion."

I looked around: the class majority was not listening—consciously. Red knew; his eyelids rose and he blinked twice. Richard and Robert were staring at snow falling past the window. Alfred was cleaning his fingernails with a folding pocket-knife. The jocks at the back discussed football. I heard a cough. Alex, a new kid scarcely able to speak English, waved slightly to catch my attention. He nodded. He knew.

10 YAKETY-YAK

Alex approached me after class. "You play chess?"
"Yep," I answered, recalling my two-hundred-fiftieth game with Robert.
"You come to my house and play chess?"
"Can't. Sorry. Tonight's poker night."
"Poker?"
"Card games. Money."
"I come?"
"You got a dollar and bus tickets home in case you lose?"
"Yes."
"Here's my address."
Friday evenings we boozed, bulled, bluffed and bet. Since the legal drinking age was twenty-one, we obtained our liquor supply from Robert's sister's boyfriend's older brother. Mother was tolerant: six teenagers were unlikely to get stoned sharing a half-pint of lemon gin over five hours. Mert played basketball on Friday, so our basic complement was a quintet—Richard, Ape, Robert, Red and me—plus a guest. As host I chose the sixth but Red, on his own, invited a seventh.
"He's back," Red informed me as we separated the oak dining-room suite, lifted out the heavy leaves and slammed the top together into a reachable, playable surface.
"Who?" I asked.
"He should have my nickname."
I felt queasy. Red and his Cree nemesis would shatter Mother's Irish crystal in one of their free-for-all fights. "Percy?"
"Not a chance," Red laughed. "Guess again, dummy."
The doorbell rang. Robert, looking pregnant, slipped past my arm. "They were out of lemon gin," he muttered. "Max got us beer and wine. Unzip the jacket. My arms are numb and my knees hurt. I didn't know there'd be so many people out tonight. I had to waddle like I was naturally fat. It's tough."
Red and I sympathized briefly while transferring Robert's cargo to the fridge.
"Halloween Apples!" Ape and Richard called as they entered.
A polite knock sounded. Alex had arrived. I ushered the group to the table and, in full view, counted out fifty-two cards.
"One's missing," Red declared.

"Not missing," a voice from the hallway declared, "just temporarily absent. As the lion said to the Christians, 'Am I too late for dinner?'" A head with carrot-orange hair poked into the dining room. "Knock, knock?"

We knew better and kept quiet. Alex didn't.

"Who's there?"

"Keats."

"Keats who?"

"Keats, David. A most humble servant, sir, if you're a paying customer; otherwise, get outta here." He stopped aghast. "Peter!" Dave exclaimed, tickling Ape's chin. "How you've grown." He slipped into a chair. "Red invited me," he murmured. "Treaty Rights."

Red's ears twitched. "'As long as the sun shines and the waters flow you may, for ceding this land, invite the white man to play poker so you can win it all back.' Treaty 7. Look it up."

I was too happy to quibble. The evening portended well. Dave was one of those free spirits who come suddenly into your life and you're never really sure how they do it. We knew he was from Newfoundland and had nomadic parents; we knew he had stayed briefly at St. John's school; we noticed his disappearance and, two years later, witnessed his resurrection.

Red riffed the cards. "Straight poker. Nothing wild. One draw. Ante up."

We chipped in and talked, hesitantly at first; no one wanted to broach the obvious: Friday evening, and we seven were dateless.

Alex thumped his fists. "Please," he said firmly, "tell me the rules."

I was dealing and recited the litany. "Royal flush beats straight flush beats four-of-a-kind beats full house beats flush beats straight beats three-of-a-kind. Got it?"

"I think so."

"Deuces wild." I caught Alex's bewilderment, flashed two fingers, saw him nod and, on the showdown, win with a 5,6,2,8,9, straight. He could look after himself. I also noticed Richard had over-bet that hand, plus the next.

"What's with the big time gambling?" I asked.

Richard refilled his wine glass, munched a handful of salted peanuts, sipped the port, and answered. "I'm fifteen. Dad's kept my American citizenship. In three years they're gonna draft me, gimme a rifle and tell me to fight atomic bombs. In three years I'm dead. Hell, tomorrow we might *all* be dead. What good's money when you're facing that?"

"You are worried about the Russians?" Alex sounded interested.

"Who isn't?"

"I'm not. When I was little boy, the Russians chase the Nazis out of Hungary. First wave were good soldiers. They tell my mother and sister to hide because animals coming. Second wave come. No boots. No guns. They steal even light-bulbs and they kill men and take clothes off women.

Important thing is: first wave—very few; second wave—many more. I think Russian good soldiers too smart to make war with America."

"And vice versa," Red concurred. "Whose deal?"

Robert scooped the cards. "Are priests allowed to play poker?"

"Sure," Dave said, "except strip poker's a no-no." He gazed intently across the table. "How come Ape stuck his fingers in his ears?"

"You said something that offended his purity," Richard sighed. "He's stopped sinning so's he'll be in the state of grace when the bombs fall."

Dave lept to his feet and paced rapidly around our circle. "I can't believe what's happened to you guys." His face reddened, obscuring his freckles. "Robert's stopped thinking of marriage, Ape's given up hearing about girls and Richard's given up, period. The only sense I've heard is from Alex."

"And me," Red interjected. "I agreed."

"Okay, so that's two with some common sense. Billy?"

"Most of Russia got destroyed in World War Two. There's no way they want to go through that—only worse—ever again. They'll let their flunkies, like the North Koreans, do the dirty work."

"Right!" said Dave, still circling. "Now suppose Senator Joe McCarthy gets elected president and decides to attack them?"

"The generals would lock him away somewhere. Like Alex said, good soldiers aren't stupid."

"Aha," Dave halted. "But suppose McCarthy was president and made Douglas MacArthur his top general?"

"I'll worry when it happens."

"You're not worried now?"

"No."

"Cor-rect! We've been here half an hour. Any bombs? No! Three guys have wasted their worry for thirty minutes. Pour me a beer. Let's play some cards."

Dave sat. He inspected Ape's chips. "House rules say you can't leave while you're ahead until the last hand's over. We're gonna discuss girls and if those fingers head for your ears I'll stick 'em up your nose. I declare Ape an involuntary listener. Anybody else need absolution?"

Ape relaxed. His voice had become even deeper after puberty. "Fire away," he boomed. "I've been needing a night of debauchery. Anyway, confession's tomorrow afternoon."

Robert dealt. "Kings and little ones. So, Dave, where've ya been?"

"Mount Carmel, on the south side. It goes up to Grade Ten. We cross the river and invade St. Joe's next year. Girls there yet?"

"After Christmas. You got girls in your class?"

"Sure. Some of them are beauts."

"Dating any?"

Dave paused and folded his cards. "No. It's sorta strange. There's three groups. One bunch is heading for nunhood; they won't date. The second bunch talks about university or nursing; they study all the time. Then there's the drop-downs."

"You mean dropouts," I suggested.

"Nope. One of them gets you alone and the next minute she has you on the floor wrestling. I'm afraid to date them. I'm too young to get married. That true what Red told me? Three Grandin Grade Nines got hitched?"

"Yeah," Richard confirmed.

"We lost two. Spooky. Quit school, find a job, get an apartment, lose your freedom. Scary."

"You mean," Red choked, "when the girls come to St. Joe's we *still* won't be able to date?"

"Oh, you can take them to school functions and maybe a chaperoned birthday bash, but beware of movies or house parties when their parents are away. In those situations, the flesh is willing and the spirit's weak."

"I know what you mean" Richard stated. "I dated a girl like that and lucked out. She took off her panties. I chizzed in my shorts. End of the fun. She wouldn't return my phone calls. Hooks, crooks and one-eyes." We considered it sophisticated to call a different poker game each round.

Red drummed his fingers. "Seems to me the trick'll be to find who the varsity girls are and date them."

"Why?" Ape wondered.

"Companionship."

"You got sisters?" Ape asked. "I have. Girls are another species. They think different. You should hear them at our dinner table."

I understood. Mother's bridge club members all talked at the same time; my poker group spoke in sequence. Double-dating would be like listening to two radio stations. And yet, I recalled, some girls at St. John's had been fun to converse with—like Patsy—and intelligently insightful—like Pauline. I started to demur but Dave interrupted.

"We shall now play goofus. Everything wild except the Queen of Spades." When we groaned, he pushed his chips to the table's centre. "Okay. Serious poker. One round of stook. Black Jack. You bet against my pile."

Alex received clarification. He had a ten showing, as did Dave. Alex bet his dwindled stack. Dave took a card. "Beat twenty." Alex flipped his face-down ace. "In my country we do not play poker but we *can* count to twenty-one."

Dave broke even on the game and passed the cards. "Please," Alex asked, "what game I play?"

"You're on a roll." I explained how to deal up-and-down-the-river and watched him harvest a fortune.

Ape shuffled the cards. "My hands've been lousy. Low-ball." He gathered his winnings. "That's more like it. Over to you, Red."

Mother helped me wash the glasses. "How did you make out?"

"We played jacks-or-better-to-open on the final round. I lost everything."

"How much did you start with?"

"The usual, a dollar."

"I spoke with Mr. Morin today. He can give you part-time work at Safeway. Your school marks have been good and it would be nice if you earned some money and bought your stepfather a Christmas present. He's done a lot for us."

The thought of spare cash excited me. "When can I start?"

"Tomorrow."

11   GET A JOB

The *Edmonton Bulletin* ceased publication in 1951, leaving me unemployed. The paper route had been a reliable source of income: $2.40 a week plus tips at Christmas. I never had to ask Mother for money—and I didn't dare: Mickey, in the kitchen one evening two years before, asked whether he could have an allowance.

"All the kids get them," was his ultimate justification.

Mother, very uncharacteristically, leaned her elbows on the table. "No son of mine expects something for nothing."

"But I," he glanced at me, seeking to double his support, "I mean we, help out. We do dishes, vacuum, dust, rake leaves, shovel snow..."

"And eat and sleep here," Mother concluded. "If you lived next door and did those things, I'd pay; but you are fed, clothed and housed by your stepfather. The least you can do is keep his home tidy."

Mickey took a deep breath; I paled and tried to blend with the refrigerator—he was about to blurt the unmentionable.

"What about that cheque you get every month from the government? That's your allowance."

"That," Mother replied, "is the Family Allowance. I earn it. Each election I work long hours for the Liberal Party. So does—rather *did*—your brother," she emphasized looking at me.

Mother was a Liberal; I, since age eleven, had been Conservative. My political conversion was effortless and basically prototypical: I was bought.

The 1948 provincial election day was sunny, hot and—unusual for Edmonton—humid. The polling station in the Robertson Presbyterian Church basement was muggy. I sat on the steps by the voting area. When citizens came in, I handed them brochures extolling the Liberal candidate's virtues. I also recycled discarded pamphlets—if they'd not been stepped upon or crumpled. A tall, distinguished, grey-haired man entered. He took my pamphlet in his right hand, thanked me, read, and returned the brochure.

"I've cast my ballot. Give this to a new voter."

He greeted my opponents further down the staircase. "Thanks, boys, you're doing a fine job." His left hand profferred two ginger ales. He opened the bottles with a multi-purpose pocket-knife. "We're in a close race." He left.

His volunteers made a show of slurping noisily and yumming loudly. I, parched, tried to ignore their belches. Five minutes passed. The door opened. I rose. The gentleman was back. He ignored his helpers.

"Your parents have undoubtedly told you never to accept gifts from strangers. Allow me to introduce myself. J. Percy Page. I'm one of the candidates. You are laboring as hard as my two friends there. Please forgive my oversight in not giving you this earlier."

He uncapped a dewy Coca-Cola and gave it to me. I knew Mr. Page had made an unscheduled trip to Carrington's Drug Store a block away. He re-examined my pamphlets. "Good worker. It would not distress me to lose."

During a lull in the voting, I dashed to the drug store. Mr. Carrington fingered two pennies from the till and streaked a thumb down the moist bottle.

"Is this the one Mr. Page just bought?"

"Yes."

"Are you a Conservative?"

"Yes!"

After the polls closed, T.J. drove me to the Knights of Columbus clubhouse at 102nd Street and 100th Avenue. We found our way to the telephone room.

T.J. peeled a printed form off a pile. "Write down the totals as the calls come in."

I soon recognized my phone's bell tone and dutifully copied numbers. Between calls I reflected: religion, in this case, Catholicism, and politics—Liberalism—were somehow intertwined. I also noticed that voters moved like a flock of sparrows: the first poll swung in the direction that the others followed.

The Liberal candidate stood in the doorway dispensing cash. "Can I count on your support in the next election?" I heard her ask my fellow receptionists. All answered affirmatively. My turn came. She held five dollars aloft. "Going to vote Liberal when you're twenty-one?"

"No," I answered, kissing good-bye to two weeks income on the paper route.

Her eyes darted sideways. I was last in line. She opened her purse. "Here's an extra dollar." She thrust the money into my hand and ushered me out the door. "We must," I heard her say to a boater-hatted confederate, "raise their pay." She didn't understand.

When J. Percy Page was later appointed Alberta's lieutenant governor I was not surprised: he had class. A partisan premier could consult him in confidence. We had learned in social studies that although politicians hold *office*, the lieutenant governor possesses the *power* to veto unjust legislation. J. Percy Page had demonstrated to me that the province was secure.

Following *The Bulletin's* demise, I earned money delivering flyers but the work was sporadic. I wanted steady income. Mr. Morin's offer seemed to be, at first, political: he and T.J. were Knights of Columbus. I was fifteen, a year shy of the legal employment age and, feeling guilty, meandered through the 95th Street Safeway and found the manager's office. Mr. Morin raised his head.

"Howdy," he greeted. "Your mother says you're not a quitter. I hope she's right. Nobody else'll go down there."

We descended a dark stairway to the basement. Bare light bulbs cast shadows behind piled cartons and heaped sacks. Mr. Morin whistled as he dragged his hand along the conveyor belt. The blackness deepened. I wondered which he depended upon most: echoes or touch. We rounded a corner. His footsteps stopped. In the dimness I saw his hand reach upward. A pull-chain rasped and a light-bulb blazed. My eyes squinted.

"This is the mortuary. You prepare the bodies for public viewing."

The work area was rectangular. Behind me the conveyor belt ended, feeding onto a twelve-foot downward slope of bare metal rollers; we had entered through a draw-bridge gap that Mr. Morin clanked shut.

"When shipments come in, unload the crates and stack them here with the other coffins," he said, sweeping his arm to the right across rows of labelled boxes. He reached for a claw hammer. "Then you pry open a casket, struggle to the sink and dump it."

On my left the cutting board and sink lay below knives slotted into a wooden wall-bracket. Light glinted off the variously shaped blades.

Mr. Morin drew a scimitar from the caddy. "Use this one for turnips and cabbage." He tapped a machete. "Lettuce and celery." The sickle was for corn. He poked a cleaver. "Watermelon and display grapefruit, when the other half's gone rotten. Paring knives, serrated blades and short rapiers. Everything the undertaker needs including," he opened a massive door, "the cooler—if you get ahead in your trimming. How do ya like our morgue?"

I tried to appear brave. "Looks more like a dungeon." My feet, swept by icy air from the giant refrigerator, slid toward a central drain. Mr. Morin caught my elbow.

"That's true," he said, flicking a switch. "This's a branding iron for sealing cellophane and, if you're not careful near the conveyor, this place has a rack." He squeezed my arm. "One other thing: you're not alone down here."

A thought flashed. Childhood terrors. The Beast in the Basement. I had long since rationalized the werewolf-bear could not exist. A lesser fear seemed reasonable. "There's a ghost?"

Mr. Morin did not laugh. "Worse," he whispered, "there's a maniac. Listen."

Beyond the gentle hum from a ceiling fan, I heard distant singing. "Roamin'... gloamin'... bonnie banks..."

"That's our Scottish fairy. If he comes around, grab a knife and keep your back to the wall. He's nuts. I thought it'd be safe to send a girl down but he snatched her boobs first time she went for coffee."

"Why don't you fire him?"

"Economics. He was off sick once and it took three men to do his job. Speaking of money, you'll get the top starting wage—seventy-seven cents an hour." Mr. Morin vaulted the conveyor. "Just remember, if the maniac comes prowling, stab first and plead self-defence afterwards."

Darkness. Morgue. Dungeon. Maniac. I chuckled. New guys have to get initiated. I recalled how Laval and T.J. had whispered and giggled after the K.C. rites for new members. Fright was evidently Safeway's *modus operandi*.

I hacked for two hours. The finished produce went into tapered wooden boxes—like little coal cars—which I deposited in the cooler. The trimmings were returned to their original crates and stacked close by the conveyor. I tossed moldy oranges and lemons into a garbage can and polished their neighbors with a moistened towel. Beets and carrots required twist-ties. Lettuce needed wrapping. I caught the rhythm of repetitive work and began to reduce the backlog. The front row cleared, I heaved a lettuce crate out of the darkness; it slipped from my grasp. I picked it up more carefully; it again crashed to the floor. I kicked the crate to the lighted area, reached for the claw-hammer and recoiled. The thing was crawling with slugs. Coffee time.

I washed my hands, raised the conveyor gate and hurried through cardboard canyons toward the other light in the catacombs. I assumed I was headed for the lunch-break tables but, gradually, my gait slowed. There was no conversation in the area, just a muted cooing and groaning. I peered around a corner. A fuzzy head was bobbing. I eased forward. The maniac was making love to the mammary cotton corners of a sugar sack. He stood, fumbled with his fly and turned two sacks upright. I retreated to my slug-infested rectangle. "What's next," I wondered, "tarantulas in the bananas?" I sat on an apple box and wondered what to do.

Mother had stressed the importance of being polite. One Saturday, in the Strand Theatre's washroom, I had been accosted by a flasher. "Aw," I said sorrowfully to the man, "too bad it's so small." I never saw him again. That retort, somehow, didn't seem appropriate for the maniac. I concentrated, lost in thought. Silence—then a small sound behind my right shoulder. I tensed.

"WELCOME TO SLAVEWAY."

I whirled around, knees bent, left forearm guarding my throat and right hand poised at waist level with knifeblade horizontal. No one was there. I cautiously checked the thin gap between the cooler and the wall. Vacant. The produce stacks? Nothing. Behind the garbage boxes? Nil. Under the sink? Silly; no way he could have gotten there. I sat down again and started to relax. Where was he? I felt a chill up my back. Of course. He had to be on top of the cooler ready to pounce, and I was facing away from the door. Another sound. This time, point the knife upward. I sprang to the centre, slipped on the drain-slope and slammed supine on the cement. Numb from the neck down. Helpless.

"CAN YOU HEAR ME?"

"Yes," I replied, urging the feeling in my arms to return faster. I wiggled my feet and wobbled my knees. Stay calm. The paralysis was subsiding and he hadn't jumped yet. Keep talking.

"Where are you?"

"UPSTAIRS OF COURSE. THIS IS URBAN. WE NEED LETTUCE."

I looked sheepishly at the squawk-box on the wall. "Right away, Urban."

At five minutes to noon, the ceiling's fluorescent fixture sputtered, then shone; it was like the superstructure had been lifted, letting sunlight in.

"Master switch," Urban explained as I munched a sandwich. "The maniac likes it dark. We humor him."

"What about me?"

"Don't worry," Urban yawned. "The boss told him a small lie. Said you're on day parole after cutting up a zoot-suiter gang on 96th Street. If the weirdo comes around, just start mumbling incoherently."

I folded my brown-paper lunchbag and stashed it in a hip pocket for Monday's lunch at St. Joe's. Urban and I went to the mortuary. He seemed impressed.

"Finish up that last stack, wait for the pig-men, and c'mon upstairs."

"Pig-men?"

"Yeah. Farmers. They feed the trimmings to their hogs. We give it all away free."

"Why?"

"'Cause while they load the trucks, their wives are shopping and the store makes money." He cocked his head. A distant tenor reverberated in the basement as the lights flickered out.

> "Have you ever been down
> to the riverside shanty,
> To watch your uncle
> on top of your auntie?"

"That man is strange," Urban muttered.

Strange indeed, but not reckless. The maniac never came calling. It was, I reasoned, advantageous for me to have a reputation: good preferably—bad if necessary.

Working after school Fridays, full-shift Saturdays and whenever the need arose, during the Christmas vacation, I had, in early January, an eighty-five-dollar surplus account with the downtown Royal Bank. The girls were due at St. Joe's and I was, I thought, ready to receive them.

12 CHANTILLY LACE

School recommenced January 5, 1953. I set my alarm clock Sunday evening for seven forty-five; the extra time was needed to brush my teeth *again* after breakfast and, for the first time in two weeks, to shave. My attempt at growing a mustache had failed: fuzz-filled gaps were more prominent than straggled whiskers. I lay in bed and mused about the next morning. Mother would be up early changing sheets and emptying hampers for Blue Monday's wash. My eyelids popped apart; would it be Red Monday instead? I went to the bathroom and faced the mirror; the acne was still under control but one dared not be complacent about pimples—they could erupt in joyful unison overnight. My selective diet was working, so far.

I had made a fortuitous discovery in October; there was a relationship between food and skin. Garishly-attired Kiwanis clowns were stopping cars and pedestrians on Jasper Avenue; the toll was a nickel, the token an apple. I took a MacIntosh home, washed it carefully and bit. A strange, cold, crawling feeling appeared near my nose. I gnawed softly, to prevent what I thought was spray from the pulp. Nothing. I chewed, and my cheeks tingled. "So," I said to myself, "that's what acne's caused by."

In the Grade Ten washroom a noontime ritual had faces being soaped, then sandpapered with industrial-grade disposable towels. Somehow, pimples seemed to flourish under those adverse conditions; but dermabrasion treated the effect rather than the cause. The apple incident induced me to think: if MacIntoshes excited sweat glands on my cheeks, what foods caused acne elsewhere? Through combination and elimination, I came to the conclusion that strawberry and raspberry jams went intact to my forehead, plums and raisins re-formed themselves in painful lumps on my nose, and peanut-butter, an old friend, had developed a new kinship with hair follicles on my chin.

I made a mental note to breakfast on black coffee and dry toast before meeting the girls. "Gentlemanly behavior," I dozed. "Put your best face forward. Treat them with respect."

Robert was on the bus. We were dressed in the officially frowned-upon school uniform: broad-shouldered, back-belted blue overcoat, plaid scarf and shirt, green corduroy balloon pants shrinking to a skin-rubbing drape shape at the ankle, diamond socks and oxblood-polished shoes in toe rubbers. Very cool.

Robert concurred with my tactical plan. "The girls will be nervous," he said.

We alighted on 107th Avenue and proceeded to St. Joe's. The walk was slightly uphill; we heard the commotion before we saw it.

A student gauntlet had formed beyond 108th Avenue. One row, lounging on the south playground's knee-high rail fence, cheered or jeered specimens scuttling to school; the other group, swaying arm-in-arm on the boulevard, emitted whistles and wolf-howls.

"Degrading," Robert tutted.

"Shameful," I agreed.

We marched between the lines of girls.

A brunette's dark eyes focused on me. "Hey, Skinny, what grade you in?"

"Ten," I muttered.

She accosted Robert. "What's your grade, Shorty?"

"Grade A," Robert countered, thrusting his coat pockets forward, "*large.*"

The left line applauded and the right side whooped.

My face became unseasonably warm; California's citrus crop was ripening. A curly-haired harasser noticed the blush.

"Wow, Skinny, make a slow circle," she shouted, pirouetting her calf-length coat into a flare. "Show us your imitation of a traffic light."

The barrage continued; I felt like little half-mitt across the street. We were ejected when new targets appeared.

"Awful," I gasped.

"Fun," exulted Robert. "Let's go around the block and through it again."

I looked back; braving the sidewalk had been foolish. I steered my friend to the school's north entrance and merged with a confused cluster.

Mert sighed. "I hear they're gonna do it again at lunch."

"In the new cafeteria?" Ape gulped.

"No," Mert added. "In the hallway near the washrooms. They've got us by the short and curlies."

"Not necessarily," stated Alfred. "We'll ignore them."

Mert's voice rose. "How can you pretend you enjoy getting your nuts kicked?"

We settled into an uneasy silence.

"Maybe," Ape brightened, "we should eat in the classroom."

Alex bristled. "That would be giving in to animals."

Red tensed. I knew something was afoot. "Animals?" Red wondered aloud. "We can be animals too, but we'll do it right. Let's show them *The Monkey.*"

"The what?"

"The Tarzan hidden underneath these overcoats. That's what they want and," he purred, "that's what they'll get. Ape will lead our wedge."

"Why me?" Ape protested.

"Because," Red explained patiently, "the honor of Neanderthal Man rests on your slumping shoulders."

We passed notes during class. Richard drew us the definitive diagram.

"Just like a football play," he whispered.

The noon bell rang. We stood silently as Easy Ed wheezed from the segregated classroom: boys occupied the new north wing; the girls were consigned to the old south. We lingered, giving *them* time to palisade the westerly lunchroom corridor.

"Ready?" Richard hunched his back. He swayed his hands past his knees.

"Set!" Mert bent his legs and shuffled sideways like a crab.

"Arooga!" Ape gurgled, head swinging pugnaciously, mouth agape.

Our simian legion lurched down the hall. Girls shrieked and scattered. We bounded through the gym door and turned, snorting, to face the female foe. They'd vanished.

Red strode to the boys' washroom; he reassumed the demented-monkey stance. "Some women" he growled, "hid in here. Who wants to show them how to use a pissoir?"

We charged through the doorway and met a screaming counter-tide.

Red grinned contentedly, "We're even."

The 38th Parallel, named after its Korean counterpart, was the truce line between our school's north and south wings. A huge invisible barrier existed from the ground floor hallway's six-inch wide metal joiner strip to the third storey's ceiling; as reinforcement, black-garbed sentries patrolled all three levels. The F.C.J.'s allowed us to see their girls only in the hallway—no stopping; the cafeteria—no mingling; and the library—no talking. School dismissal hours were cleverly staggered. It was, we found, easier to meet girls from the public high schools miles away. An effect the nuns had not foreseen was that their wards were sipping Cherry Cokes with boys from Victoria and Westglen while we Catholic suitors were still receiving homework assignments.

We boys were like a theatre audience; the transplants from St. Mary's were almost as distant—and unreachable—as figures on a movie screen. We sat at lunch nibbling sandwiches *in lieu* of popcorn, and watched the actresses perform. Their show was, in essence, a split-screen triple feature starring probables, possibles and postulants. Each troupe wore distinctive costumes, we discovered; our enlightening lunchroom conversation began innocuously.

"Just think," Alfred mused, chin cradled in his palms, "every single one of them goes naked twice a day."

Ape excused himself and sat at another table.

"Yeah," Robert interjected, "my sister doesn't wear any of those clothes underneath her nightie."

Alfred stared, as if hoping he would be endowed with Superman's x-ray vision. "Not even panties, I'll bet."

"Naw," said Robert. "They're put on after the morning bowel movement."

He was ordered to sit with Ape.

Richard appeared fascinated. "I wonder why they choose what clothes they'll wear."

"In my country," Alex said, "there is no choice. All girls wear uniforms like them." He pointed at a secluded corner table.

We craned our necks. Five demure damsels were having a garden party; feet square and knees together, they dissected their sandwiches with knives and forks, smiled sweetly at each other and sipped milk from glasses, disdaining the waxed cartons and drinking straws in use at other tables. Their uniforms, noted by Alex, were similar: tightly-buttoned starch collars pointed to aproned smocks like those at Safeway. But in the store, all workers wore the same utilitarian outfit; at St. Joe's, the asexual clothing seemed out of place. Mert dismissed the group.

"Nuns-in-training," he shrugged.

I perked my head. Mert had imparted valuable information: girls were sending visual signals across the silent gap between us. The corner groups's axilla-high aprons clearly declared the area between their shoulders and belly-button out of bounds. Right! So whose pectoral areas were still in play? Was it the girls wearing sweaters or the ones in blouses? Not wishing to alert my competitors, I eased into the subject.

"Why," I asked nonchalantly, "do they wear blouses opening toward the left?"

"Because, dummy, they sit in the passenger seat at drive-ins," Red responded.

"How about blouses that button down the back?" Snuffles around the table told me I should have kept quiet.

Red regained his breath. "Most guys undo bra-hooks better with their right hand."

More table thumping. Father Mac materialized.

"What's all this levity?"

Alfred raised his hand. "We have to speak loudly to Alex, sir. A bomb blast in Budapest perforated his eardrum."

"Hardly reason to applaud."

"He burped through it."

Father Mac parted mumbling.

Richard resumed the conversation. "What's with those little collars some of them wear above their sweaters?"

"Okay." Mert looked around and lowered his voice. "Here's the scoop from the guys on the team. Those..."

"Dickeys, I think they're called," said Alfred.

"Yeah. There's three kinds of dickeys. The starched linen ones mean the girl'll date, but that's all. You might get to hold her hand. Chantilly lace means she's looking and wants to get married after Grade Twelve. Watch out. The fuzzy collars are made of rabbit fur..."

I didn't hear what else he said; my attention was diverted to the girls' tables. Jenny was wearing a furry collar *with a blouse*. I turned to Mert.

"What's it mean when they wear a sweater with no dickey?"

"Going steady," Mert replied. "They don't need any more necking."

The bell rang. We folded and pocketed our paper lunch bags; they were reused—not bought—in the Fifties. Red sidled over.

"Wanna see chestnuts disappear?"

I wondered if he was into magic tricks. "Dazzle me, please, Houdini."

"Check that out." He gestured toward two buxom females. Both wore heavy, ornate pendants that impressed their sweaters, and us. They entered the washroom.

"Some trick. You knew they'd go there."

"Sure, but not for the reason you think. Wait a minute."

A moment was enough. The girls emerged, relatively flat-chested. Their pendants were modestly hung at clavicle height.

"Two chains," winked Red. "One for the nuns and one for us."

Life was more complex than I had thought.

13 AT THE HOP

We asked Angelo to be our spokesman, mainly because he had the most club and sport crests on his blue St. Joe's sweater sleeves: we wanted someone not accustomed to rejection. He looked older than the other Grade Elevens—and most of the Twelves. We Grade Tens waited expectantly in the hall near the girls' principal's office. Angelo emerged.

"No Valentine's dance."

Richard was angry. "Did you remember to say *Saint* Valentine's?"

"Yeah. Mother Sedimentous didn't bite. She also refused the Mardi Gras idea."

Richard became disconsolate. "No Easter orgy?"

"Nope. Look guys, gimme a week. I know a parish priest who's still thumping the Rosary Crusade. I'll tell him there's hundreds of teenagers looking for a hall to pray in..."

Thus was born Club Saltatio, the place hearts beat faster.

The teachers tried to wheedle information from us. They'd sensed our mood change, eavesdropped on conversations and intercepted notes. Something, they knew, was up—but they didn't know where.

Father Kelly paused during his lecture. "I can understand your boredom with this, considering you're all looking forward to the Trocadero." We stared.

Father Daly attempted the chummy approach. "I understand Chic's Bar-B-Q is the place to be on weekends." We rolled our eyes in disbelief.

Father Mac was, as usual, direct. "We priests are accustomed to hearing sins. If the police pick up any of you I will, personally, volunteer to extract your confessions." We snickered, when he wasn't looking.

Father Fee used reasoning. "Come on, I don't think you guys'd look good with vertically-striped suntans." We laughed.

They never suspected one of their own was involved. Frank Schneider knew. "Have fun at St. Andrew's tonight, and don't worry." He peered over his horn-rimmed glasses. "I won't squeal."

Robert and I felt drums and bass vibrating the entranceway. Our hands stamped with indelible ink, we pushed into the gym. Trumpets and a saxaphone blared. The piano player was pounding keys wildly but his music couldn't overcome the din. We nudged through the crowd toward Richard and Alfred.

"Hi, y'all," said the former Texan.

"Jolly good show, wot?" added the Brit.

"Met any girls?" I asked, scanning the expectant lineup along the far wall.

Embarrassed silence, then the band launched into Glenn Miller's *In the Mood*. Couples jitterbugged across the basketball court. A sickening realization stunned me.

We only knew how to waltz.

14 ALL I HAVE TO DO IS DREAM

I squinted in the July sunlight. Urban had summoned me from the dungeon to unload yet another green truck stuffed with fruit and vegetables. Edmontonians descended in summer on Safeway's Vitamin C stocks like grizzlies search for berries in the spring.

"Calving time!" Urban called as he unbolted the truck latches. He had been raised on a farm and, I suspected, yearned to be a cowboy. "Comin' down the chute!" Urban delivered crates with an obstetrician's dexterity and sent them along the portable conveyor belt. "Slaughterhouse!" designated bulk produce to be swung onto low-wheeled dollies destined for the retail area. "Feed lot!" told me to boost crates onward for trimming or inspection prior to sale. I didn't need instructions regarding canned foods and drygoods—they were the maniac's responsibility and careered untouched along the endless inclined plane to Safeway's nether region.

Gustav, the produce department's manager, stood aside and ticked the list on his clip-board; he chose not to sully his hands. Urban skate-boarded down the rollers and leapt to the floor at attention.

"Is goot, *mein herr*?"

Gustav's high forehead furrowed; he was counting. Urban and I leaned against the banana baskets; a light breeze tickled our sweat as we awaited the dreaded final tally. One missing item meant reversing the belt and stacking every box for reinspection—Gustav deigned not to enter the basement.

"Vun box lemons is missink. Should be two."

Urban flicked the squawk box switch.

"Do you hear me? Check the lemons."

"Two," barked the reply.

Gustav was mollified. Urban and I went downstairs into darkness.

"How'd he see to count the lemons so fast?"

"He didn't."

"But..."

Urban paused at the freight elevator. "Look, I bitched when Gustav did his first and only recount. He won't let me come down here and check 'cause he thinks I'd lie. Trusts the maniac, though."

"I still don't..."

"Reversing the belt breaks the maniac's concentration so we worked out a code. Now, what'd I say to him?"

"Do you hear me?"

"No, *deux* you hear me. *Deux*. That told him to count two boxes."

"Suppose there should have been six lemons and eight oranges?"

"*Six* what you're doing. Check the lemons and oranges *toot-huit*! Foolproof. Gustav hasn't caught on yet. At best, he thinks he can't count. At worst, I sort of suggested he might be having *petit mal* seizures like my cousin and the way to check is by seeing if the clock hands move too fast. Mr. Morin's caught him staring at the wall more than once; he figures Gustav is having absence attacks."

I wondered, trimming cabbage, whether daydreaming counted as an absence attack.

Grade Ten had been an academic success but a social disaster: I'd passed, unattached. Faced with three alternatives—study, play, or study *and* play—I had chosen the third but was shunted by events to the first.

Apart from the inability to jitterbug Forties style, I was disadvantaged by not having, or being able to drive, a car. Several Grade Tens, sons in wealthy families, had their own automobiles; these classmates triple- or quadruple-dated girly carloads weekend evenings, competing disdainfully with those of us who relied on the bus. I was, in retrospect, glad I had not ingratiated myself with the drivers: Eddy, who cruised the biggest car, and Jenny, his instant steady date, both flunked Grade Ten after having zombied through the school term's final months.

I lacked female companionship and, adding insult to ennui, the poker club had disbanded. On the final Friday a majority, distracted by sports or the frantic pursuit of females, failed to attend. Red's mother had prepared a buffet and baked special prizes for the winners. After Red, Alex and I had played a few cursory hands, she presented us with doggie-bags.

"You three," she remarked calmly, a thin waterline visible along the dark eyelids, "have your priorities right. I'm satisfied."

I cracked a celery crate, continued trimming, and caught the rhythm of repetitive work: my grandfather's solution for slowing down the world was to retire to his garden and dig—I felt a kinship with his memory.

Since Grandpa's death I had been untouched by five summer polio epidemics. Although popular belief associated polio with unwashed fruit, I didn't feel uneasy working with produce—most of it appeared to have been picked and packed by machines; the rest, I rationalized, could not have been harvested by palsied workers.

Alone in the basement corner, I enjoyed the freedom and control a solo job affords. Energy bursts preparing lettuce were followed by leisurely sitting sessions to polish mold off citrus fruit. I also learned sales techniques.

Urban, when the California strawberries arrived, said, "Put all the baddies in one basket and send them up with the rest." Curious, I wasted a coffee break to check the sales floor. There in the showcase was the putrid container and, nearby, four bright and fresh baskets. Sales were brisk. Urban kept busy supplanting the snapped-up quartets. "People," he remarked, "like to hoard what they think is rare."

My wage had increased to seventy-nine then eighty-one cents an hour. The bank account was growing but I still didn't have sufficient money for dance lessons; I doubted I ever would: the quoted cost was ten thousand dollars.

The voice on the telephone had sounded excited. "You have," she said, "been selected as possible prize-winner. What is the capital of Alberta?"

"Edmonton," I replied suspiciously.

"Correct. Now for the grand prize, what's the capital of Canada?"

"Ottawa."

"Congratulations, you've won three dance lessons. Absolutely free. When can you come to claim your prize?"

"How about Friday at five?"

"Perfect. Could I have your name please?"

I resumed eating dinner and related my good fortune.

"It's a scam," said T.J.

"Beware," Mother added.

"Don't worry," I reassured them. "I'm almost sixteen."

T.J. relaxed. "Then any contract you sign won't be valid—not 'til you're twenty-one."

"What makes you think I'll sign something?"

"You'll see." T.J. sipped his coffee and stared at me.

The studio had a famous dancer's name in neon lights over the doorway. "Surely," I thought, "*he* wouldn't be associated with fraud." Stung by the Saltatio humiliation, I entered as a willing participant. A busty blonde greeted me.

"Let's start with a fox-trot. Follow those footprints on the floor."

We stumbled through an awkward shuffle.

"Great!" she exclaimed. I wondered whether she enjoyed having her toes stepped on. At least I hadn't caused her stiletto heels to fracture.

The music restarted. I halted. "Look, Ma'am, I'm really interested in learning how to jive."

"That comes later. This's a waltz. Let's see how you do." She pulled me unnecessarily close. Our thighs brushed. Her fortified brassiere dented my chest. My feet, distracted by the above-knees activity, continued to assault her insteps.

"Fabulous," she exclaimed. "You've got great potential but," she saddened, "jiving's not included in our free program. I'll introduce you to Ruby."

The diminutive, frizzy-haired redhead sat behind an imposing desk. She reminded me of my Aunt Lil, a company woman to whom business varied between routine and tedious. I was wary.

"He's interested in jiving," the blonde stated, easing me into the office with a touch on my behind.

"That takes time," Ruby shook her head. "You first have to learn the basic steps. We've got yearly memberships but that's for older folks. I think you'd be interested in a life membership." She gestured at pictures on the wall. I recognized a classmate's father. "These people attend all our parties and meet members of the opposite *sex*," she emphasized. "The yearly dues are one thousand dollars. After ten years everything's free. Just sign here and you're guaranteed fun forever."

A white contract for green money. I recalled my childhood friend, Arthur, offering to trade tattered, coverless comics for newly-bought issues. I stood, in disbelief, frowning in disappointment. The blonde barred the doorway, squaring her shoulders for maximum mammary effect. Hardball time.

"Sorry," I said looking at her forehead and pointedly ignoring the chest, "I don't want *cheap* lessons." They gaped as I walked out.

That evening T.J. had been ecstatic. "You'll fare better with driving lessons. I'll set it up with the A.M.A. on Monday."

Urban interrupted. "Grunions," his parched voice rasped. "The mob craves grunions and corns on the knobs."

"Howza strobbries 'n lettoochie doon?"

"Hokay, but the blushin' baby turnips are gettin' lonesome."

I sent green onions, cob corn and radishes along the conveyor and began trimming more lettuce.

The Alberta Motor Association's training classes were attended furtively: jacket coat collars up to avoid identification, we resembled the Gem Theatre's patrons on adults-only night—ashamed that something *everyone* knew was beyond our ken.

The instructor sensed our embarrassment. "There is," he said, "a difference between driving a car and steering it. We'll start with showing you how the motor functions, then how the clutch interacts with the driveshaft, and—finally—how to *master that machine*." Hands on hips he stared at us. The room became warm. As if on cue, we roused and shucked our jacket disguises: ready to work; eager to learn. The instructor folded his arms in satisfaction.

We probed the internal combustion engine's secrets and graduated to the street sign seminar. A noisy argument caught my attention.

"It's forty-seven."

"Sixty-nine!"

I studied the diagram. Clearly, the red and green dots outlined the numeral fifty-eight. My confreres were adamant. I remained silent. Our mentor eased over.

"Trouble?" he asked.

Paul traced an incomprehensible four and seven. Andy outlined an impossible six and nine.

"What do *you* say?" the teacher inquired.

I tried to gather saliva but my tongue had developed tentacles. I hoped the instructor could lip-read.

"Fifty-eight, sir," I sputtered.

"Right! These other guys are color blind. Come on, fellows," he beckoned. "Special instructions are required before we let you loose on the roads."

Paul's world was a black and white movie. Andy's perception stopped at gray and blue. Neither could differentiate a green traffic light from the red. Neither, I mused, would survive Tipperary Hill.

"You," the instructor pointed, "must not take anything for granted out there. Assume every driver is Paul, Andy or female."

I had no difficulty remembering the prejudiced admonition: the one female at St. Joe's who owned a car was polyandrous and an enviably skillful driver—at most times.

Yvette swung her Bel-Air to the curb. I lowered my thumb.

"Always room for two more," she shouted.

Robert and I packed in among a glowering back-seat foursome. Rubber squealed as the car accelerated. Yvette was happy.

"You are all," she exulted, "in my power."

Then she began to sneeze. Violently. Uncontrollably. I looked askance at Robert's Wildroot; he sniffed my Brylcream. Yvette's head bucked beneath the steering wheel. Oncoming traffic darted sideways. Yvette convulsed, eyes red, tears pouring down her cheeks. The car lurched. Pedestrians scattered.

The vehicle died at an intersection. Yvette lay back gasping. Robert and I exited.

"I think," he had said philosophically as the Bel-Air receded, "girls are allergic to us."

I slid into the A.M.A. car and stared at the twinned controls: half an American motorcar had seemingly been welded to a British right-drive model. Louis, the wizened, white-haired, safety valve wheezed behind the other wheel and slammed the passenger door.

"Okay," he sighed, "scare me to death."

I admired Louis' teaching method: put the car in gear, set your mind in neutral—and listen.

"The guy ahead is weaving, so ease to the left rear, time your move, then burst past; those curbside trucks yonder: watch for kids chasing balls; there's someone in that parked car's driver's seat—he's gonna open his door; a green light two blocks away means slow down 'cause it'll be amber when you get there; aim for the distance but glance at the road cracks. Got distracted by that girl on the sidewalk? Try and explain it to the policeman who's checking the car you rear-ended." And so it went.

We braked on the steep road near the Legislature. Last lesson. Louis had something planned.

"Depress the clutch, put on the emergency brake and shift your foot to the accelerator." He leaned back and paralleled himself with the incline. "Now climb that hill." I killed the motor. "Try again." I ground the gears. "Once more." We sailed over the crest. "You're ready."

Test day. Parallel parking. Obstacle course through downtown and across the North Saskatchewan's bridges. The examiner was inordinately fastidious: still stung, I assumed by the defunct *Bulletin's* front page features.

The *Bulletin* in its death throes tried contests and sensationalism to boost readership. Under the province's lax laws, the *Bulletin* had obtained valid permits for a dog, a William E. Goat, and a stuffed duck, named Mort Anses. The animals were pictured proudly sitting behind a sports car's inviting dashboard. The Social Credit government, wrenched from lethargy, instituted on-the-spot driver testing.

We took the final pass up 110th Street near the Legislature. The civil servant patted his watch.

"Hurry up," he urged. "I have to be back in five minutes."

"Can't, sir," I replied, recognizing a tree-shrouded blue sign near Grandin. "This's a school zone."

The examiner marked his score sheet. "You've passed." He relaxed and switched on the radio.

"*Yes, we have no bananas*," the baritone boomed. Urban's voice. I was back in the basement.

"Come off it, Urban. You know they're not stored down here."

"Yeah, but I feel like singing."

"Gustav's been fired?"

"No such luck, but in a way better. The union's coming."

"So?"

"So the good news is our wages go up fifty per cent."

There was an obviously awkward gap in his jubilant recitation.

"Okay, Urban, what's the bad news?"

"The bad news is that at $1.23 per hour we can't afford to employ you any more. You're gonna be laid off in September."

"Thanks a lot," I snarled, slamming a machete into the carving board.

"Wait! Don't take off your apron." Urban's speech became a whisper. "Mr. Morin's offered me the top produce job at the new 124th Street store. How'd you like to be my second-in-command?"

I had seen the construction. Three blocks from home. No more cycling. No more stale sandwich lunches. "You serious?"

"Want me to sign a contract?"

"Nope, Urban, I'll take your word."

"That's more binding," he assured me, "than any piece of paper."

I believed him. Urban had an abiding disdain for paper. At first, I thought he resented Gustav's carbon copies, then, one day on the sales floor, the truth emerged.

"It is," he surveyed a swirling wave of shoppers, "one gigantic rip-off here."

"How d'ya mean, Urban? Like bananas at two pounds for twenty-one cents?"

"Nuts," he replied. "Safeway's really nuts. People come in here, hand over bits of *paper*, and we give them *food*. Ever try eating a dollar? Ever nibble a nickel? But give your $1.05 to us and we hand you *ten pounds* of bananas toted all the way from Central America. We are," he smiled, "getting taken by those clever folk." He paused and thought. "On the farm we supplied our own meat. Got the herd stocked. Birthed the calves and piglets. Fed them. Cleaned up the barn. Nursed the cattle through illness. Watched 'em grow, then zip," he drew a finger across his throat, "got them ready for the table. Year-round job. People here get it all done for one little piece of paper."

"But money..." I started.

"Money," Urban frowned, "is nothing. It's paper. What you use it for's what's important."

I wriggled the machete. Stuck. More force would break the blade. I stood back. Something was amiss. I flicked the squawk box. "Urban."

"Yo."

"Why're you happy the union's coming?"

"Because, my friend, the wife and I'll be able to buy a home on our own land."

My friend. Laval used that term. Laval and Urban were both of French descent. And yet my brother-in-law had implied land was valueless. "Urban?"

"Still here."

"Anything else besides a house and garden?"

"How old are you?"

"Almost sixteen."

"Kids. I'm changing my pay cheque into a bunch of kids I never thought we could afford. Strange, isn't it?"

"Huh?"

"How paper from trees comes alive again."

I levered the machete free. The ceiling seemed lower. The screws were tightening. The restless feeling returned. I found my pocket-watch. Quitting time in five minutes. I cleaned the cutting board, polished the knives, doffed my apron and left the basement three steps at a time. The bike ride home was a blur.

"Did you leave early?" Mother asked, inclining her head toward the kitchen clock; she never pointed at anything.

"No," I said, rapidly verifying my watch's accuracy. "I just felt like cycling."

T.J. appeared. "Energy to burn?"

"Sort of."

"You'll need it. Just before you arrived there was a telephone call—*from a female.*"

My expectations didn't leap. T.J. had a tendency to tease.

"Thomas," Mother clucked. "Nuns are not *females.*"

"How true!" T.J. roared as Mother sputtered a disclaimer. "But even so, one of them's interested in your son."

I dialed the number, counted two buzzes, and alerted at the click.

"Mother Sedimentous speaking." Evidently hell, even disguised as 'Hello', could not enter the discussion.

"Yes, Sister?" My manners lapsed back to St. John's; the nun ignored my *faux-pas.*

"In the St. Joseph's Cathedral poster competition for advertising Perpetual Adoration your entry won, did it not?"

"Yes, Mother Sedimentous." The reply was superfluous—I knew she knew Mother Igneous had cued me to the "Calling All Parishioners" alarm clock motif.

"You have been chosen, ordained as it were, to be the editor for our St. Joseph's High School year-book."

"But we don't have a year-book Sister, I mean Mother."

"There is to be one. Put your mind to it over the coming months. I have spoken with Elaine and she will be your co-editor. May we count upon you?"

Elaine? A fellow St. John's alumnus. Fiercely independent—and pretty. The challenge was irresistible. "Certainly."

"I am pleased." She would later be confounded. "Good-bye." Obviously, "God be with ye" was acceptable conversation.

A year-book? Interaction with the girls? A crack in the box? Officially approved? With Elaine!

After supper I rummaged through Edward's and Norine's Green and Gold University of Alberta volumes. I balanced a load to the bedroom and extracted the latest, a 1942 edition. I checked headings, noted the format and paused at pictures showing partying adults. There were, I reasoned, in those remote photographs human beings that survived high school and went on to better times. There was, perhaps, life after Grade Twelve. I set the year-book on my lap.

"Mickey?" I summoned my brother from the lower bunk. "You got a feeling the world is closing in on you?"

"All the time," he laughed, kicking my slats.

"C'mon, get serious. You guys feel a kind of tension?"

"Not me, 'specially 'cause I know how to read. Mom taught us the good way. But you should see those 'Dick and Jane' kids struggling. They're lost—and they're gettin' mad. I got a feeling somethin's ready to bust loose real soon."

My little brother had capsulized the situation. I also wondered what was going to happen. I closed the book and, clasping the worn covers, doors to both the past and future, drowsed as the bedside alarm clock ticked.

15   HEARTS OF STONE

The Korean War ended in July, 1953; the 38th Parallel remained intact at St. Joe's that autumn. We also had our version of Europe's Iron Curtain—a huge folding door divided the gymnasium so male athletes could not observe females at practice and vice versa. Seeing one's schoolmates in an abbreviated uniform was, evidently, an occasion of sin: the nuns were bent on preventing lustful, hairy-thighed boys stampeding the smooth-legged girls into the washroom or, worse, catching them and indulging in an orgy on the basketball court.

Elaine stirred her cocoa. "I know it sounds silly, but that's how they think."

"Absurd," I replied. "You mean to say the nuns consider us guys are all sex fiends?"

"I'm afraid so," she said, crossing her legs beneath the table—I recognized the sound of nylon crossing nylon and suppressed the urge to lunge.

"Ridiculous," I emphasized, watching her interlock fingers behind her head. "Don't they give us any credit for being civilized." I made a conscious effort to keep my hands on the coffee cup and away from her sweater.

"Nope, the good sisters regard you as one stage up, at most, from cave-men."

"Unreal," I remarked, amazed that with both hands firmly on the table, I had begun to count the change in my pants pocket.

"It is unreal. They're living in another world, but it's sort of consistent with the seventeenth-century habits they wear. 'Stick with the good old days' seems to be their motto." She sipped the chocolate, her eyelashes sending a Morse code of long and short blinks—I regretted having concentrated my scouting studies on semaphore.

"How'd you like *From Here to Eternity*?" I asked, sensing an advantage.

"Great movie. I just loved the beach scene. That reminds me, I should be home in bed. Waitress?"

The girl brought our cheque. Hot chocolate had increased in price.

"Uh, Elaine," I mumbled, manually recounting my change.

"Don't worry," she said. "Dutch treat tonight."

We boarded the bus and headed west on Jasper Avenue.

"The year-book's at the printer's now. Wonder how it'll turn out."

"Just like we planned," Elaine replied. "That's the trick—let them censor the obvious while you slip by the subtle stuff."

"And keep a straight face all the time."

"True," she agreed. "The key is to be sweet and innocent outside and crafty underneath. By the way, speaking of sweet and innocent, gimme your transfer." She tore up the ticket and pulled the next-stop bell cord. "I'll see myself home, thanks. This's your stop, I believe."

"Maybe," I thought, watching the bus depart, "she likes older guys." No, that was improbable: St. Joe's lightning-fast grapevine hadn't associated her with anyone. Even Norm, Grade Eleven's ultra-cool zoot momentarily lost his composure when, mouth agape, he saw Elaine and me entering the theatre. He oozed over, spinning his yard-long watch chain like a propeller.

"Howzit doon, baby?"

Elaine's eyes flashed at the whirling gold circle. "Norm, you look like the ass-end on a motorboat so why don'tcha go jump in a lake."

"Duzzis mean we're through?" he moaned.

"We were through, *baby*, when you were born."

Norm persisted. "You two goin' steady?"

"He ain't steady, he's my brother."

Norm's jaw dropped again and I fed his maw some popcorn. In the darkened theatre Elaine and I were warned by the usher to stop giggling.

There was a nugget of truth in what she had said: in battling the nuns we were telepathic twins.

M. Sedimentous had enlisted M. Metamorphous for moral—literally and figuratively—support. I met Elaine outside the windowed office. She peered through the glass.

"The M. and M. show," she murmured. Her tongue passed slowly along her lips.

My tongue also flicked. "Let's eat them up."

We swooped into the office brimful with enthusiasm and ideas. The nuns stood and bade us to sit. We sat. They towered over us. I didn't have to look at Elaine—we'd lost the first round.

Mother Sedimentous took the advantage. "The year-book will, of course, be dedicated to The Blessed Virgin and will have as its theme the religious life." She proferred typewritten sheets. "Archbishop MacDonald has kindly answered your request for a spiritual message, as has Bishop Savaryn."

"But we never..." I started.

"Then you should have," M. Metamorphous tutted.

"In addition," M. Sedimentous continued, "we have a printer's plate depicting The Queen of Heaven. The statue's photograph will be a fine front cover."

"But..." Elaine sputtered.

"The valedictory messages shall extol seminary and convent vocations and, when graduates are unsure regarding their future, the brief biographies shall hint at a preference for celibacy."

I didn't know whether to laugh and walk out or turn red and argue.

"We have here a list," M. Metamorphous interjected, "with the names of Edmonton's Catholic merchants. They are to be approached for advertisements."

I could hear my heart pounding. Exit time. Knees braced. Palms flat. Elaine's hand gestured slightly across the desk. Okay, kid, over to you.

Elaine shook her head. "No, Mother—and I'm sure Bill will agree—*that's not enough*. Television's coming to Edmonton next autumn. There's hardly any other news on the radio or in the papers. Just think: we'll be able to *see* Pope Pius say mass. We'll be present in the Vatican. There should be some year-book reference to TV."

Beautiful. She had hit them at a blind spot. I couldn't imagine either nun listening to CJCA or nestled in bed with *The Journal*. Perfect. I relaxed. The wedge was in; all we had to do was pound it home. Elaine tilted her head. I caught the pass.

"Uh, Sisters," I deliberately absent-mindedly reduced their rank, "since we dedicate every day to Mary through our 'prayers, works and sufferings', it'd be redundant to assign her a year-book. After all, it seems kind of inappropriate to have The Blessed Virgin at the start and ads for clothes and houseware at the end. Father Daly's retiring; let's give him the honor. When the guys check the ads and prices most of them'll decide not to get married."

Fluster time. Cloistered conference. Agreement. We'd taken the second round: TV and Father Daly were in; the B.V.M. didn't make the cover.

A tentative truce reigned over the succeeding months. M. and M. weren't sure what we were up to—and they suspected the worst. Strangely, they saw sin where there was none while blatant bamboozlements blew right by them.

Elaine and I had to explain that the graduate who liked "Size 3 peas" was expressing, not his bladder, but a preference for an agricultural delicacy.

And that the basketball photo showing girls' legs should not have brushed-in long skirts appended. "Legs are legs," Elaine said nonchalantly. "Everybody's got them."

Or that the joke about a matrix being two mattresses did not warrant censoring. "We are," I remarked, "in the *Separate* school system."

So, preoccupied with the subliminal, the nuns ignored our triumph, the ultimate symbol of rebellion: Mert's photo.

"We've just gotta get it in," Elaine gasped.

"Not a chance," I choked. "They'll never allow it."

"They will," Elaine reflected, "if the caption's right."

I studied the photograph. Mert, the coach, was surrounded by his girls' baseball team. "How about 'Lady Killer'."

"Great!" she shouted. "The nuns'll think the bat between his legs is for hitting helpless females who couldn't play ball. One more reason to be celibate."

The photo passed inspection with only a cursory glance; I was surprised: Mert's three foot phallus had been immortalized.

I mounted the steps at home. Our year-book would be, I reflected, a curious hybrid—medieval morals contrasting with Fifties' flagrancy. My urge to telephone Elaine had to be suppressed: calling anyone after eight o'clock was considered rude. I dialed her number the next morning.

"That was fun last night. Like to go out next Saturday?"

"No," she said. "I'll be busy."

"How about the next weekend?"

"Still busy."

"Doing what?"

"Looking for a guy somewhere."

"I don't qualify?"

"Nope. You're kinda too close. We've been through it all together. I want somebody new, somebody different."

"From another tribe?"

There was a long silence. "How," she whispered, "did you know that?"

"I've been watching Red and Sue."

"Exactly," Elaine breathed. "That's what I've been searching for. We're so alike anything between us won't work."

I accepted defeat. "Good luck in your search, buddy."

"And the same to you, *buddy*."

We both understood. The telepathy continued after I recradled the phone. To grow, to mature, we had to break free from St. Joe's oppressive environment. I patted the telephone. Elaine would survive. But did I have the same innate toughness? My thoughts flashed back to the 115th Street gang. Same ages. Same experiences. Same schools. Yet, despite our world's tightly-structured path toward priesthood, Red had found Sue.

16 YOUNG LOVE

It began at a basketball game. St. Joe's was losing—the Victoria coach ordered double-teaming on Mert. Red and I, the poker club having disbanded, had bought tickets through curiosity: what, we wondered, was the attraction in seeing Sep's representatives once again humiliated? At half-time, I grumbled at Red; the waste of valuable study time had been his idea.

"Pain," I said, noting the scoreboard. "All I feel is pain."

"Excitement," he shushed me, pointing toward Vic's cheerleaders. "Get a load of who's on the floor."

I appraised the kick-line. Vic girls were doing an intricate drill. Females from another world. Enticing but belonging to different faiths and therefore beyond approach. Red gestured.

"Check the third from your right."

I counted and watched. The girl was stunning, both in appearance and self-confidence. Shoulder-length black hair whirled in sensuous rhythm with the muscles on her arms and legs. She threw her pompoms skyward at the finale and I scanned the line: she alone did not wear a bra. "Red," I cautioned, "remember you're Catholic."

"Yeah," Red's voice deepened. "But more important, she's Blood."

I looked at the girl's bronze skin and prominent cheekbones. There *was* a resemblance. "You're related?"

"I think so, way back."

Red descended to the gymnasium and beckoned the cheerleader. Their animated discussion was interrupted by the referee's whistle.

We disregarded the third-quarter play.

"Well," I asked, "are you her cousin or something?"

Red's concentration focused on his look-alike. "She's not Blood; she's Peigan."

"Pagan? C'mon Red, have a little compassion for the Protestants."

I was subjected to a withering stare: Red usually did that when he doubted my sanity. "You dummy," he chuckled. "I'm Blackfoot. I thought she was Blood but she's really Peigan."

I remained confused. "'Fess up. Who is she?"

"Sue."

"Sioux?" At last enlightenment glimmered.

"Yeah," said Red, his answer trailing off into a contented disassociation. "I'll introduce you when this slaughter's finished." I peeked at the scoreboard and winced: Vic's red-clad team was engulfing St. Joe's white-uniformed soldiers. It was Custer's last stand all over again.

The game score in those frugal times was chalked on a blackboard. There also was no official clock and we had to guess the time remaining. Red squirmed, anticipating the final buzzer; I had never seen him more agitated. My distraction became intolerable.

"Red, do me a favor. Go to the washroom and get those ants out of your pants."

"I will," he smirked, "if you coat your head with honey so they'll have somewhere else to go."

The remark stung. Until that moment he had been a confederate, an equal member in the gang; now he was establishing a distance from us palefaces. I recalled meeting his father: braided hair, buckskin clothes, moccasins; I recollected my grandfather saying Red's dad had class. Maybe, I rationalized, my friend was finally finding himself. His hand found my shoulder.

"Sorry, I shouldn't have said that."

I thought, then laughed. "Don't worry. As a come-back it was too good to pass up."

Red exhaled in relief and gently punched my arm. "You're a sweetie."

The game ended. Sweat dripped from Sep's players while light perspiration glowed off the Vic team. Most cheerleaders mingled with athletes on the court; Red's new acquaintance met us in the stands.

"Sue, this is Bill."

Soft speech contrasted with her firm handshake. "Any friend of Red's ...is immediately suspect."

I liked her.

Red feigned astonishment. "You don't trust us?"

"One learns to be wary," Sue smiled, "around Toad Hall."

Red guffawed. I couldn't catch my breath. Overwhelming mirth. Sue's assessment of Vic was, somehow, apt.

"Toad Hall?" Red croaked.

"I named it," Sue deadpanned, "the first day. Its grass was covered with black-leathered creatures squatting on their haunches in the sun; they had wart-sized unsqueezed pimples, buggy eyes, slimy heads, and were..." she herself began to laugh.

"...blowing bubble gum," Red exploded.

"Precisely," Sue said.

I tried to restore decorum to the discussion. "Sue, your team beat us tonight."

"Because," Red snuffled, "they could jump higher."

"And dribble better," Sue added.

"One step up from drooling," Red explained.

"Look, Sue, here at St. Joe's we've got Norm. The greasers aren't all at Vic."

"I know Norm. *Everybody* knows Norm. At Toad Hall, Norm is the norm."

I tried a different tack. "You gotta name for Sep?"

"Not yet. I'm working on it. Something to do with horses."

"Horse High?"

"Close. Describe the typical St. Joe's female."

I mentally scanned the hallway. "Saddle shoes and pony-tail."

"Very good. *Saddle* and *pony*. Now, on dance nights they tippy-toe on high heeled shoes that look from the front and sound on cement like..."

"Hooves," I conceded, recalling sounds preceding the bread, milk and ice wagons in my childhood.

"So you've got horses. How about riders? The Sep guys' jackets've got colored shoulder flashes the same as..?"

"Jockeys," I remembered. "Blue Boy" was etched in my consciousness.

"And when they strip down before Phys. Ed. classes what're they wearing?"

"Jockey shorts."

"So for the games they put on..."

"Jock straps." She had me.

"St. Joe's," Sue reflected, "is like the Calgary Stampede in miniature: a bunch of horny guys getting bucked off frightened fillies."

"Horny?" I questioned.

"Like toads," Sue concluded. "Vic and St. Joe's have a lot in common."

Mr. Flaherty flicked the gym lights. The place was deserted. Red waved and we helped the janitor stack chairs, fold the gallery and sweep the floor.

Walking to 107th Avenue, I fell several paces behind. Red and Sue halted at the west-bound bus stop—I was surprised: was Sue seeing Red home? We boarded. I sat at the back. Sue motioned me forward.

"You are," she stated, "our chaperon."

After transferring at 124th Street, we headed south and exited at 103rd Avenue. I was becoming uneasy. *Was* she taking him home?

Sue shook Red's hand and pecked his cheek at 122nd Street. "That's my house. I'll make it from here."

We watched as she disappeared in the darkness. A door clicked. The porch light went out.

I was incredulous. "She lives there? How come I've never seen her?"

"She cycles to school in the spring and fall and runs to Vic in the winter," Red marvelled. "That's how she got those chest muscles." He departed, humming.

I walked the block home. The house was unusually bright.

"Laval's here," Mother announced, "with something for you."

Laval approached, holding a bundle. "Your dog Spot ran away, when was it?"

"New Year's Eve, 1950."

"*Voilà*," he proclaimed, flipping the cloth's corner, "his replacement."

A frightened, reddish-coated cocker spaniel tried to hide in the blanket. Laval thrust the dog at me; I avoided tiny claws and supported the wriggling body. He settled, secure in my arms.

"He's yours," Laval said.

"It's late," Mother cautioned. "Take him, the blanket, and some newspapers to the basement. You can get to know him tomorrow."

In bed, I heard muffled yelping, donned my slippers and eased past my parent's bedroom. Mother heard me.

"Go back," she said, "and get your alarm clock with a hot-water bottle. He'll be more secure."

I was puzzled but followed instructions. Clancy—the name seemed inappropriate—nestled contentedly and quieted. I felt warm, watching the little fur ball fall asleep.

Strange, I thought back in my room, Red had found true love while I had to settle for the puppy variety.

17 WHAT TO DO

I had become a guardian: without benefit, or the benefits, of wedlock. I acquired an infant that needed toilet training and schooling about worldly dangers; Clancy began singularly dense but progressed to an amazing astuteness. Laval's gift, in turn, became a subtle sign that I would be more comfortable as a parent than a Father; insight arose through a change in my mother's comments—less and less, as the pup and I began understanding each other, did she mention priesthood. Instead, Mickey received her attention.

Freed at home from maternal pressure, I was better able to withstand Father Mac's sales pitch.

"Give me one good reason," he demanded, "why you shouldn't become a priest."

"I like girls, Father."

He ushered me from the office and grasped the nearest neck; iron fingers turned my head. "The sex lecture's Monday. Be there!"

Monday had been chosen, I supposed, because our teachers could cold-shower us with homework for four days; a Friday talk would have left the weekend for red-eyed deflowering.

Monday arrived. Father Kelly tried to teach social studies, his statements scarcely heard above the classroom's expectant buzz. He slapped a ruler on the blackboard. Momentary silence.

"So," Father Kelly inhaled, "the Cold War comes down to this." He let out his breath and peered at us. "We find ourselves between two paranoid giants. I take comfort from one fact: no civilized human would vaporize the Hermitage in Leningrad or reduce to dust the Smithsonian in Washington." Seeing his comments largely ignored, Father Kelly left early.

Spare time before the sex lecture. I looked around the room. Our all-male class ran the gamut from disengaged nonchalance through quiet apprehension down to nervous agitation—the latter expressed in what we called "concentration".

Concentration was an exercise in self-mutilation, a minor form of suicide. In it, the object was to rub away, with a thumb, skin over the opposite first web space below the wrist. Novice concentrators brought subcutaneous veins into view; true addicts proudly displayed the deeper, pulsing artery, exposed and vulnerable. It was a way some chose to tempt death: Frank Schneider had cued Robert and me to concentration's significance during the Grade Eleven beard-growing contest.

"Are you guys in this competition," he joshed.

I fumbled with my hall locker door. Robert tried a diversion.

"Look," Robert exclaimed, holding aloft a tattered lunchbag, "the mice've been in it again."

Mr. Schneider was not deterred. "Mice get through that inexplicable hole the manufacturers left in the locker tops. The beasties feel it out with their whiskers in the dark. So, where're *your* whiskers?"

"Hiding," hoped Robert.

"They're here," I said, brushing my upper lip. "You just hafta look real close."

Frank put his arms across our shoulders. "Don't worry," he said, "you're lucky; you'll mature late and live long. The winners of this contest'll be fortunate to see their fortieth birthday. Have you noticed? The concentration guys've got five-o'clock shadows; they sense the end is near and wanna get it over with."

The clock hands eased toward ten. Still no teacher. Alfred, Richard, Alex and Red were mute. Ape, transferred to our class, was irritated: East-end guys in the back-row seats were sending inflated condoms in his direction. I chanced a surreptitious look—the toughies resented anyone staring at them. Penny loafers below white socks under blue jeans covered at the belt-line by a V-necked sweater exposing the neck-high white T-shirt; the cap on their uniform was hair trimmed to a brush-cut on top but worn long on the sides into an occipital duck-tail. Black leather jackets, not entrusted to lockers, draped over chair backs. The group had an aura exuding supreme confidence. If a teacher didn't show—there were rumors they were drawing straws—Norm would likely volunteer his expertise.

The doorknob turned. Our French teacher entered to give the sermon on mounting. Mr. Lachambre staggered across the room and steadied himself against the desk. From the third row, I detected a distinct alcohol aroma; on any other day he would have been fired. I could imagine his secular associates spiking the coffee and pouring on praise: no one, popular belief inferred, knew more about female innards than those of Gallic descent; he was the laity's unanimous choice; another drink, further flattery and off you go to the lion's den.

Mr. Lachambre's eyes were doing an unnatural dance. Strange, I mused, how pupils in his sockets and the classroom were both twitching with anticipation. His chin bobbed slightly. The time had come. Silence.

"First, never show up for your honeymoon in thish condition." He grinned as applause erupted from the back rows, then pointed to a waving hand. "Yes?"

"Sir, my little lamb's always in heat. Can't keep her satisfied." Two condoms exploded. "What can I do?"

Mr. Lachambre's smile vanished. He drew himself soberly upright. "Anyone who has intercourse with an animal is...beneath contempt." He wavered to the door, about-faced and reappeared. I recognized Father Mac's riding crop giving a final push. Mr. Lachambre rocked to a stop.

"Second, you mush avoid impure thoughts until you're married, then anything goes."

"Anything?" echoed the chorus.

"Within reason. Just remember," his eyes clicked into focus, "a woman is not a seminal spittoon."

Another hand went up. "Sir, sometimes it's hard..."

"Yeah," approved the gallery.

"...I mean difficult to keep impure thoughts away when she's unfastening her bra."

"Say a Hail Mary if there's time, otherwise try a short ejaculation."

The hand went down. "You're right, sir, that'd end it."

"Messy, messy," disclaimed the back-row.

"Shaddup, you guys," Ape shouted. "I wanna hear this."

Norm was unsympathetic. "Whazza matter, beetle-brow...?" He sprang toward the door as Ape leaped to dismember him. Chaos. Mr. Lachambre turned from the uproar and leaned his forehead against the blackboard. Norm slammed into Father Mac. The priest was purple.

"What," he roared, "is this levity?" He grabbed Norm's cheeks near the ears. Painful. "I said levity!"

Norm had been terrorized once too often in Latin class; he responded out of reflex. "*Leviti, levitorum, levitis, levitas, leviti, levitis.*"

Father Mac threw him against the wall. Norm's head cracked and he slumped, unconscious.

Angry mutterings from the class. Ear-twists, parotid-pulls, hair-tugs and occasional strappings were one thing; beating into insensibility was quite another. Father Mac knelt down.

"Norman?" he pleaded to the lolling head. "Norman?"

The same thought hit us simultaneously. We gelled. "*Normani, normanorum, normanis, normanas, normani, normanis.*" Outright rebellion. East-end and West, North-side and South united against the foe; we dared him to take us on.

The principal motioned to Mr. Lachambre. Together they eased Norm to his feet and guided him through the doorway; it was difficult to determine who was supporting whom.

Thus ended the sex lecture.

18   ONLY SIXTEEN

Sixteen. Half-way through the teens. Five years on either side from puberty and legal adulthood. While seven was the age of reason, sixteen was supposedly the age of enlightenment. And yet I didn't realize what was actually happening to my generation and its world until the lightning bolt struck on a muggy summer evening in 1954.

T.J. had been delayed at the office and supper was on simmer. Snooze time—I'd worked hard that day: Urban and I had fine-tuned the 124th Street Safeway's produce department to the point that vegetable displays were covered with moist burlap before we met the bag-laden last customer at the door; on the way home I noticed grey-black clouds boiling in from the west.

Tummy rumblings merged with distant thunder. I was drowsily counting one-gorilla, two-gorilla, between light and sound to determine the distance from the storm centre when FLASH-BOOM, my picture was taken with a cannon camera.

Mother, Mickey and I ran to the back yard, expecting to see our roof aflame. Mickey pointed. An alley telephone standard was split and smouldering.

Work crews arrived the next day and, in the rain, erected a new pole; it was different. In contrast with adjacent poles, lathed into symmetry from giant logs, the new structure was a recently-barked young tree, tapered at the top as if shrunk by the drizzle. Back in my room, the image bothered me. Edmonton, growing rapidly since the 1947 Leduc oil discovery, had been forced to compromise in telephone pole design. A nascent thought surfaced and jarred me: new was not necessarily better. I sat back, stared at the wall calendar and tried to reconcile my conflicting observations of life in the Fifties.

Deeply ingrained in the Canadian subconscious is a feeling that change, no matter how drastic, is reversible. The idea derives from our experience with four distinct seasons: however brutal the winter, soft summer invariably succeeds. Storms subside and the world reverts to normal. But—and this concern disturbed me—the summer air in 1954 breathed over a different landscape than was present a year earlier. Time was passing.

I swiveled in my chair. Height markers on the bedroom door frame denoted progress; I was growing but so, I reflected, was the world and therein lay the problem: our schools were teaching Forties methodology whereas what we needed was Sixties survival training. For the first time, I understood my classmates' restlessness.

The oilfields' wealth brought people, both the industrious and the unsavory, to Edmonton. On leaving the house, we routinely locked up. I recalled that in 1945 I had, for no good reason, slipped the button lock on our 115th Street home's front door and returned from school to face a tremendous uproar: no one knew where the key was hidden; it had not been used since we moved in.

Petroleum evidenced itself during the Fifties, both over and on the streets. Hand-cranked cars vanished, replaced by those with key ignitions. Robert's father bought a Hudson and told us kids it was the car of the future. Square-nosed trucks sprayed oil by-products on gravelled residential streets to reduce dust; the service was terminated when citizens complained the tar marks on carpets were more difficult to remove than film on furniture.

Parking meters appeared downtown; the universal response was outrage: an unfair tax, people said, on those who would support local businessmen. Then, whether by accident or design, the first major suburban shopping mall—with free parking—was built at Westmount.

City politics had a certain constancy—the oldest candidates were routinely elected except for Fred J. Speed, a perennial mayoralty hopeful who was summarily disregarded by the electorate; his mistake, I assumed, was using a 1920's studio photograph for his promo ads. It made him resemble a silent movie star; he'd not acknowledged the talkies had arrived.

Conversely, silent movement became the vogue downtown: chatty operators with hand cranks in downtown elevators were replaced by impersonal numbered buttons; most customers preferred the security of adjacent stairwells. That summed it up: a technical step forward countered by literal steps upward. People were dubious.

Mother, however, had no reservations about her pressure-cooker. "Cuts cooking time in half," she proclaimed. The rubber-rimmed top was secured on the squatty cooking pot; a warning whistle perched at the apex. She turned on the gas jet. We waited. Noises of distant bubbling. Ominous silence. Sudden explosion through the rubber safety valve. I picked potatoes off the ceiling. "Mashed?" I inquired.

"It seems we have no choice," Mother replied.

T.J. was not impressed with Bird's Eye frozen foods. "These peas," he stated, "would gag a flock of starving crows."

Nor was our seemingly immutable Catholic religion immune to passing fads. Father Peyton, an American, launched the Rosary Crusade with a slogan: "The family that prays together stays together." The ulterior motive was Russia's peaceful conversion; the effect in our home was open warfare over Mickey's and my tendency to speed along and slur syllables. I thought the controversy was silly and confronted my stepfather. Why bother to enunciate when *silent* prayers were heard? T.J. countered by affixing a clashing blue Crusade plate on his green automobile's front bumper. I felt embarrassed riding even to church in a new car flaunting old values. It could have been worse: Crusade antenna flags, Marian door decals and—worst of all—luminescent B.V.M. dashboard statuettes. I couldn't image curb-cruising.

The Fifties evolved, at first, in concert with the decade's gas-guzzling cars whose engines' voracious appetites mirrored our own cravings. We kids remembered wartime food rationing and postwar entertainment taxes so everyone indulged at the Burger King and Starlite Theatre drive-in havens.

I phoned Margie. Attractive girl, but flawed by being the Legion of Mary's school president. Yes, she had nothing planned for the weekend and would be happy to *double-date*. I called Red. "How'd you and Sue like an orgy at the movies? I've got the car Saturday." Affirmative. I redialled Margie. "It's arranged." My hand paused on the cradled receiver. Red as a chaperon? Apprehension. Recalling our childhood capers, I knew he'd have the evening plotted.

I curbed the car. Red slid in, wearing a brown buckskin jacket and puckish grin. I recognized the sign.

"Something's up," I remarked resignedly.

"Congratulations," Red grasped my hand. "That's the first step to a successful date."

"You know what I mean. What's your devious mind come up with? Filthy jokes for an entire night?"

Red fell backward. "Me? I'm as pure as the driven snow."

"That bad?" I recalled the dirty brown slush stirred by cars on Edmonton's springtime streets.

"Worse," he chortled.

We cornered to Sue's house. She came down the stairs. White leather coat with intricate beaded designs in front and sensuous, flowing fringes on the sleeves. Something *was* up.

Sue swept into the back seat. "I hear your date's a bit prudish."

"Sort of," I agreed.

Red snuffed. "She says grace, I mean last rites, over the cafeteria's hamburger."

I decided to beg. "Look, could you guys do me a favor and keep quiet?"

"Quiet it is," Sue said.

"Not a word," Red added ominously.

I parked at Margie's and went to the door. She insisted I meet her parents. We chatted in the parlor. Her father nodded. My date donned a cloth coat and we went to the car. Red and Sue were in the back seat distanced by a broad expanse of cushion. Both were expressionless.

"Margie, this's Red and that's Sue."

"How do you do?" Margie inquired.

No reply, just straight-ahead stares.

Margie entered the front seat with trepidation. I turned the ignition key; her hand met mine at the gear-shift. "Are they," she whispered, pointing a thumb backward, "...alive?"

"Sure," I said, trying desperately to gain the advantage. "Watch them; they've gotta blink sometime."

We wheeled to the Starlite. I didn't bother asking our chaperones to contribute their admission fee. We bumped onto an inclined ramp as the sun set. I reached out and attached the speaker to our window. Margie was nervous; I hardly heard her whisper.

"They haven't blinked yet."

The show started. A musical. Credits rolled. Margie spoke.

"Doris Day's the greatest, don't you think?"

I muttered agreement. Silence from the back seat. The movie's prologue. Story develops. Still no motion behind us. The characters gather on the screen in an unnatural manner and begin to sing. Instant action from the back row. Sudden groans and ecstatic coupling; mumbles and fumblings throughout the song. The music ends. Red and Sue snap back to separation.

"Are they," Margie asks, "your friends?"

"Yeah," I reply. "Doris Day turns them on."

Next number. Same uninhibited response. I try a casual stretch and dislodge her glasses. She ignores my arm and clears steam off the windshield with a Kleenex.

Further dialogue, then more music. Animated gyrations in front and behind. Margie is immobile. Terrified. I brace on the pedal and turn to reassure her. The sound track vanishes—I've stepped on the clutch rather than the brake and the speaker wire waggles helplessly as our car rocks to a halt in the gully. Margie is outside.

"'Scuse me while I powder my nose."

A Margie-like figure exits the concession stand, runs to the gate and boards a taxi. We wait. Sue speaks for the first time in an hour.

"I guess we're not invited to the wedding."

I watch the taxi's dome-light disappear. "Thanks, you two." I meant it.

I was deciphering tiny figures in my math log book when Father Mac beckoned me to the hallway. Had Margie squealed already? I followed him to the second floor's north window and rapidly calculated excuses. "In spring," he peered, "a young man's fancy turns to thoughts of..."

I gazed at the playing field and tried a dry-mouthed, noncommittal answer. "Baseball."

"Precisely." He looked down at 109th Avenue. "Traffic poses a hazard when students cross to the diamond in spring and the gridiron in autumn. I want that road closed."

My penalty was to be hard labor? Pick-and-shovel on the gravel bed with a wheelbarrow to build barriers at either end? I thought about Red. "All by myself?" I winced as Mac's right arm shot out. His hand held a little metal gadget.

"Count cars."

"That's all?"

"The city will shut the road down when council sees the total."

"Suppose there's hardly any?"

"Then," he smiled malignly, "we have proof few people would be inconvenienced."

"Why me, Father?"

"'Vengeance is mine, saith the Lord,' but *He* didn't have Mother Sedimentous to contend with. You were identified. It's the least punishment I could conceive." Mac *had* mellowed.

The tedium was not in vain: a fenced 109th Avenue met us when we returned in September to Grade Twelve.

The chain-link was our principal's last hurrah—in effect, his monument. He withered into the school's background leaving other clerics the job of making their recalcitrant classes conform to the system: Mother Sedimentous led the charge. But the world was changing and we were determined—despite hell-fire religious retreats and Rosary Crusades—to keep pace.

19   JENNY, JENNY

Grade Eleven boys had been sequestered in four rooms—teachers changed classes; we stayed by our desks. In Grade Twelve we were reorganized into three groups. Mr. Schneider explained the shuffle in racing terms: he worked the tills during summer vacations.

"We looked at your track records, calculated the odds and placed bets on future performance. Certain of you are running hard with goals in sight, knowing the immediate reward's a full feedbag but the long-term prospect's being put out to stud and living happily ever after. Then there's a bunch that've given up, died in the stretch; their fate's the glue factory but they don't care 'cause quitting's easier than lathering up a sweat. Finally, we decided to corral off the broncs; it's okay to buck certain new or old ways but those guys'll break a leg and get shot rather than accept anything. Look around and figure which group you're in."

I wished Sue had been present: Horse High it was.

Frank inferred we weren't the rebel broncs so I checked my classmates. Mert and Ape were in the class but Robert and Richard couldn't be seen—both were smart. Had *I*, in the teacher's estimation, been demoted to the also-rans? I sought Mr. Schneider after class and received an enigmatic answer.

"You aced Grade Eleven," he said. "Pace yourself for the departmentals. Take a night off now and then. Don't burn out at the three-quarter post."

No hints, either, at noon. Easy Ed, Robert stated, had given their class a similar pep talk.

Richard restored some perspective. "I think," he philosophized, "the teachers've got money riding on the finals."

We thrived on the competition; strangely, our teachers did not. Father Mac took sick leave, never to return. Father Kelly resumed parish work. Tiger lasted part of one physics class. Easy Ed clutched his stomach and was gone for three months. Father Fee became principal and enlisted, for the first time in three years, a substitute teacher who was female. My class was alarmed: the departmental exam results determined who could enter university. We decided to let her know she was in command of our unruly mob, because we couldn't afford any more free study periods. The plan was almost flawless.

She entered and, as intended, met a melee. Paper planes flew among erasers, chalk and spitballs. Deafening noise, but we heard her bird-like chirp.

"Class!"

Scramble to our seats. Brush hair back. Sit upright. Hands on the desk-tops. Quiet. Attentive. Ready. Great confidence-builder for the neophyte.

She perched on high-heeled shoes, her arms and hands trembling. "I've heard your reputation, and I will tolerate no nonsense."

"Yes, Miss," we replied, having noted the ringless left hand.

Her eyes darted right and left, to the back and to the front. No one moved. She had not expected the easy conquest. "Is that understood?"

"Yes, Miss."

She remained sceptical and seemed at a loss for words. "I," she began, before clearing her throat, "I..."

Just then a light breeze from the open window dislodged a paper airplane from the light fixture over her head. We remained motionless. The plane made a lazy circle and zipped under her nose. She screamed out the door.

Our next substitute sat at the rear. "I never took Latin," he said. "Teach yourselves."

The class protested. Father Fee listened.

"Okay." He sounded determined. "Frank and I'll double our lecture schedules; you guys appoint a class supervisor for each subject. It'll be a half-hour for intensive instruction by us and the same time for homework, and question-answering, by your designates."

With three weeks left in the term, I sensed we were ahead of schedule, took Mr. Schneider's advice, and decided on occasional time off.

Athletics, particularly football, were out: any head jolt resulted in a crashing three-day migraine headache. I chose the chess club.

Alex had been vanquished by Bill from the other class. Bill and I met in the final and battled to a draw.

"No matter," said Mr. McEleney, whose typing and shorthand classes allowed him an early lunch and time to referee the noon-hour contests. "St. Joe's sends two representatives to the city finals."

Westglen, Eastwood, Varsity and Scona were summarily eliminated by St. Joe's and Victoria. I was not surprised: Ron, who had lived kitty-corner from me on 117th Street in 1947, was the Vic duet's leader. We had both grown up in the Oliver community's tough environs. I spoke with Bill.

"You take the other guy. I'll handle Ron."

Bill was at our table in an amazingly short time. "Suckered him with the four-move gambit." Ron had no objection to the interchange—our game was well underway and he was winning.

I studied the board. As white, he was one move ahead and had pressed the advantage. But his defense contained a potentially fatal flaw: after castling his king he had not wasted a turn shifting a king's pawn ahead. His rook was positioned for the final assault while the king occupied a boxed-in alley. Still, Ron's forward forces were on the offensive. I counted. Five moves and he had me.

His knight swung around to finish the attack. I swept it off the board with my queen. "No," said my hesitant hand. Too late. His bishop swooped in and my queen was gone, a devastatingly irresistible take-out.

"Game's over," said Ron.

I smiled and shook my head with eyes fixed straight at him. He appeared conciliatory.

"Look, you've lost. See the board, I've... crapped out."

The bishop's move had left a clear path downward for my rook. A slow-motion slide to the king's row captured his rook. Checkmate.

Bill examined the championship cup. "That queen sacrifice," he marvelled, "was the stupidest move I've ever seen. How'd you come up with it?"

"In street fighting, the best punch is when your fist goes backward first."

Bill, having grown up in the east-end, understood.

The jocks meanwhile had taken the city's football championship. Ape's running won the final—opponents and team-mates were stepping stones toward his goal. The squad didn't mind. Richard was limping and gingerly patted a bruise on his hip.

"Ape's winning touchdown," he proclaimed proudly.

Then the invitation came from Calgary: St. Mary's had won *that* city's title. A provincial showdown? Sure! And, uh, since there's no snow yet in Calgary, do you mind playing here? No problem! The team'll go by bus and the fans'll arrive by train. Hang onto your Stetsons: we're heading down!

The nuns initially refused to sanction the trip. Single girls two hundred miles over the horizon? Unthinkable. But the female students' union branch prevailed: their Calgary counterparts would help fund buses taking girls to the game and, with head-counts, transfer them afterward to billets at the F.C.J. convent. In the morning, buses would carry the unsullied virgins from their Calgary haven to the Canadian Pacific Railway's depot. And besides, St. Mary's cheerleaders would be at the game. Why should Edmonton's team be handicapped? What could possibly go wrong?

Boisterous boys and garrulous girls boarded the C.P.R. train at the 109th Street and Jasper Avenue station. Excitement, and wisps of alcohol vapor, filled the air. When the train stopped at Wetaskiwin, we discovered the coach-cars kept moving if we rocked them side-to-side. At Lacombe, lemon gin hip flasks took their toll. Red stood.

"I gotta go to the can. Will you excuse me?"

"Take off."

Red waited. "I need your seat-mate's permission."

Robert was asleep, mouth open, dried saliva on his lower lip.

"Granted *in absentia*." I snarled, turning to watch stubbled fields speed past in the twilight. Red was back. "That was fast."

"I'm goin' to the next car down."

"Line-up?"

"Yeah. The washroom astern's too fishy."

"Somebody barfed a tuna sandwich?"

"Nope. Give you a hint. What's got four legs and two hungry pussies?"

"A momma cat's in there?"

"No, dummy. Jenny said Yvette needed a car to attract guys and was a nobody without it."

"So?"

"They're both in the men's biffy."

"And?"

"Having a contest to see who's the best seminal spittoon."

"Jenny's winning?"

"Behind, you might say, two-to-one. Word has it Yvette could mow a lawn by duck-walking over the grass."

"You indulged?"

"Not a chance. I'm saving myself for Sue."

"How could she know?"

"Randy bragged he did them both."

"So what?"

"He's got the clap."

Buses, with nuns riding shotgun, met our train at Calgary's station. We reached the stadium as the half-time gun sounded. I thought for a moment Randy had been executed. A cheering gauntlet lined our team's path to the dressing room; they were in front with a five-point touchdown plus convert while holding the Calgarians scoreless. We settled in the stands to relish victory.

St. Mary's won 15 - 6. Our consolation prize was a dinner reception at the church hall. In the centre of beef country, we expected steak; they served us cold-cut ham and turkey.

"Oink and gobble," sniffed Alfred, shoving his plate aside. "I refuse to accept the Hun's hospitality."

"Amen," Richard agreed. "I'll be walking bow-legged for a month. But that's nothing. They stomped Tim's throwing hand."

Alfred was merging pink and white meat into a cricket-ball-sized missile. "Then, not content, they deliberately dislocated Ape's middle finger in the fourth quarter's first scrum."

I set down my fork. Potato salad made excellent glue.

A cherubic priest stood and tapped his microphone. We anticipated the cliché and loaded up.

"It's not whether you win or lose but how you play the game that counts."

"Hold fire," ordered Richard, gesturing toward the podium. Our assistant coach was sitting beside the priest and there was no way we'd subject Bernie Faloney, the Edmonton Eskimos' all-star quarterback, to a meatball barrage. We watched Bernie sip coffee and silently applauded when a hostess, demurely clad in a beige skirt-suit with matching felt hat and veil, refilled his cup.

The priest droned. "Thus, in future years, we will look upon tonight as water under the bridge, flowing onward to the eternal ocean."

Bernie pushed back his chair and went to the lavatory.

"It's time, gentlemen," said Alfred.

The priest sat. Simultaneously, the Calgary group began chanting.

"We want Louise! We want Louise!"

Puzzlement. Had they hired a stripper? Not likely; a young priest was at the microphone. He rendered a quite-acceptable Maurice Chevalier imitation.

The last notes had scarcely died on the walls when the chant resumed.

"More Louise! More Louise!"

Randy rose. "We want Yvette, and Jenny too. We want..."

Pandemonium. Dead birds flew again and pigs got wings. The young priest was undaunted. "Thank heaven, for leetle..." thunk, right between the eyes.

We billeted at the Knights of Columbus clubhouse. Alfred's melodious voice broke the darkness.

"Avery bit of cheese seemed to covair ze priests."

We were totalled.

Back to Edmonton and work. Fee and Frank held after school classes reviewing old exam questions.

Jenny died when Yvette's car crashed into a bridge abutment; her chum perished two hours later. Their funeral had an aftermath—Jenny's father went home, loaded a pistol, and blew his brains out.

Nothing much else happened in Grade Twelve.

20   THE GREEN DOOR

A robin twittered annoyingly from the leader spike on our front yard's blue spruce. My left eyelid opened and snapped shut as I flopped face-away on the pillow. Damn! With dreams consistently in color, I was having difficulty keeping a red-breast tint off Father Fee's clerical collar. What *was* wrong with us guys? Did an awards night justify the havoc we'd inflicted on St. Joe's? My feet found slippers and I went downstairs. The telephone buzzed four times, its fifth ring cut short by a familiar voice's drowsy hello.

"Red? Let's go hug a mountain."

Silence, then–"Right!" The receiver clicked. I returned to the bedroom and packed my suitcase. Ten days until university commenced. Ample time.

Red unshouldered the tent, dropped his sleeping bag and shucked a knapsack. "One problem, who's got wheels?"

T.J. refused to loan his government-subsidized car. Ape declined the trip having decided Latin study was more important. Red had an inspiration.

"Try Keats, he's back from Campion College."

I phoned. "Still got your jeep?"

"Sold it."

Despair. "Too bad. We gotta get to the Rockies."

"I'm in."

"How come?"

"Bought an old Packard," Dave said. "Seems the previous owner didn't know how to clean sparkplugs. The motor died and he figured he was unloading a lemon."

"You got it working?"

"Like a clock. We'll need one more tourist."

"Why?"

"Big car. If it gets stuck, three guys'll hafta push."

"Who'd you suggest?" The deference seemed proper.

"How about the wild Hungarian that took my poker money?"

Apprehension grew as we crossed Canadian National Railway tracks to the Calder district's soot-darkened small homes. Alex was a recent immigrant and would be vulnerable to the rigors presented by Canada's wilderness.

Alex, comfortably reclining on three bundles, greeted us at the curb. He loaded the down-filled sleeper and a duffle-bag.

"What's in the valise?"

"A coal-oil lantern and propane stove with grill, of course." Alex seemed surprised. "In Europe, one does not disturb the forest by gathering wood; each log might be a home or food for many creatures."

Red was intrigued. "So we camp, cook our meals, pack up, leave and there's no sign we've been there at all?"

"None. In one day, the grass under the tent is again standing upright."

Red whistled softly between his teeth. "*That*," he said, "is civilization."

I caught his wonderment. "*The light in the night* keeps glowing?"

"You got it," Red answered quietly. "Let's head west."

Dave's car ticked along the segmentally paved, two lane Jasper Road. Frost-cracked asphalt alternated with gravel, dust and potholes. Wheels bounced and we swayed; our journey resembled a train trip—except for harrowing runs past farm machinery being driven sluggishly along the roadside. At a coffee break in Edson, Dave tossed me the keys.

"Take her into Jasper. I'm gonna relax and admire the scenery."

I was flattered. "You sure?"

"No, but I'm tired. We're over the worst part. From here, the road's on bedrock and there's no farming. Just steer and follow my directions."

"I think I can find the mountains, Dave."

"Seeing them's one thing; getting there's another."

The road hugged an escarpment edging the McLeod River flatland far below. We turned a curve. A truck approached.

"Rockies in sight," observed Red.

"Wheel right!" Dave ordered.

I swung the Packard along the road's narrow shoulder. The truck and a sedan, side-by-side, whizzed past, the Chevrolet occupying our just-vacated lane. My knees were quivering.

"How'd you see that car?"

Dave slouched, and closed his eyes. "I didn't. Always assume some idiot'll try to pass on a hill. Clear sailing from here. Wake me at the park gate."

Jasper's foothills, unlike the bald knolls between Calgary and Banff, had a certain levelness: trees on the crests were stunted and plump; poplars and evergreens in the valleys had long, bare trunks and bushy crowns struggling for a share of sunlight. The visual effect was gentle undulation rising gradually to a rock wall's massive face. The fortress looked impenetrable except at one point: a vertical mountainside, ground by glaciers eons before, signaled the Athabasca River's break in the parapet. Fir and pine were clustered below the sheer cliff and merged with deciduous trees growing beyond the high peak's shadow. A thread-like gap, our road, gradually widened as we approached; the emerald door was opening to the sanctuary.

We hadn't intended a stop at Miette Hot Springs but a bighorn sheep flock straddling the junction obstinately refused to move. Red tried to sound jovial.

"They're telling us something." His tone changed. "Turn left up the trail."

Dave and Alex pitched our tent by a tumbling stream near the chalet. Alex volunteered to cook; Dave crawled into a sleeping bag. Red surveyed the adjacent mountain after supper.

"Let's go," he said.

He and I ambled toward bushes on the clearing's edge. Red swept a branch aside and revealed a well-trodden deer path. We climbed the mossy slope to a rock grotto. It was exactly as he had described during midnight discussions around our scout campfire's glowing embers: a secret, magical place where one *knew* that we, the trees, the earth and mountains were all the same stardust long ago. We sat and experienced the strange combination of tranquility and strength enveloping us. Dusk came. The sky darkened, then flared with more stars that I had ever seen. Each distant sun seemed to radiate warmth; together they joined the mountains in welcoming us.

Reality returned swiftly the next morning: the tent was vibrating with a drenching downpour from foggy, low clouds. Dave sounded irksome as the racket on our roof persisted.

"Why're the squirrels stampeding?" he protested under his pillow.

The rain did not abate. I held a cup through the tent-flap: enough water for brushing teeth but not a sufficient amount for cold tea. We struck our tent, greased down the winding road to town, and checked into a motel cabin. Coaxing flame from sodden logs in the fireplace, I heard Keats coaching Alex—Dave's idea was to resurrect the Hungarian's accent.

"Clerks at the liquor store'll go outta their way to serve a foreigner." He tapped talcum on his subject's slicked-back hair. "You get the booze and I'll drive the getaway car. Only rum'll save my toes from gangrene."

They left, and returned empty-handed. Alex was apologetic.

"I said, 'I vant rum', so the guy behind the counter wrote down hotels where rooms are available."

In their absence I'd charred hamburgers held in the bread-toasting grill's metal jaws. Such was brunch.

During our excursion I was uneasy: subconscious impressions were forming but I hadn't yet grasped a pattern.

At Maligne Canyon I saw rushing water sculpting bedrock; at Mount Edith, I heard stones rumbling off ledges where skittish mountain goats pranced from one shrub cluster to the next. Insight arrived during our drive south.

The Jasper-Banff connection was a single lane dirt road. Boughs and leaves brushed the Packard's roof and sides. Dave braked—a grazing moose blocked our path. Alex reached over and pressed the steering wheel's centre.

"Away," he shouted. "Get away."

The bull turned. Challenged by our car's horn, he lowered his antlers and pawed the ground.

Trapped. A sweaty trickle descended my forehead and I rolled down a side window. The moose feigned his charge—I didn't care: better to be cold-skewered than steam-cooked. We waited.

Though the sky was clear, thunder echoed. I craned and found a gap in the trees. Work crews were blasting a mountain's flank, carving the path for a new highway. The moose, distracted, barged toward its new competitor.

We drove on to the Athabasca Glacier. I got out of the car and stared. Since my last visit nine years before, the icefield had receded, exposing glacial moraine. A new landscape. I slumped, elbows resting on the hood: the mountains were changing and being changed; did any immutable reference point remain in the world?

That night I shivered in my sleeping-bag. Dave had decided a cooking shelter, with its log roof, concrete floor, and stove, was the ideal place to bed down. He didn't think the absence of glass above the waist-high walls would be a problem. Wind whistled and whirled off the nearby gigantic icefield; I had never, even during mid-January's *Bulletin* deliveries, been colder. I scrambled out and stoked the stove. Futile. The metal was torrid; air an inch away numbed my fingers.

Red roused. "Are we," he asked plaintively, "in heaven? It sure ain't hell!"

Dave sack-raced to the stove; Alex chose to roll his cocoon nearer the fire. Red leaned around the shelter's doorway and imparted bad news.

"Can't reach the tent," he chuckled. "There's a family of black bears inspecting our car."

He rummaged out the toast rack, extracted coals from the stove, and blew a log fire into life on the cement floor. Heat bathed our icy limbs; the conversation turned to a natural topic.

"Girls," Dave declared, "are a different species."

Alex discarded his English fluency. "Zey are, uh, how you Americans say, very strange." He opened his palms to the flames; the accent disappeared. "I can't understand them. For instance, why do attractive girls think they have to put on layers of make-up and get their hair curled for year-book pictures?" He turned to me. "Explain please, mister former-editor."

"It bothered me," I conceded. "I hardly recognized some of them in the photos. It's peculiar how somebody that stuns you in the hallway turns into a Grecian statue when the lens clicks."

"Crap!" Red butted in. "She's still the same."

I countered. "Suppose Sue walks down the aisle. You're gonna be married in a few minutes. She lifts her veil..."

"And...?"

"She's got her hair done in ringlets."

Red retched. "You win."

"Speaking of marriage," Dave said, "I hear a bunch of grads got hitched right after school ended."

Alex snorted. "Foolish. They think life is as simple as the cafeteria's five-cent soup and eight-cent milk. They forget about rent and babies."

We hunched closer to the fire, comforted: arctic wind on our backs was inconsequential compared with problems now being faced by those who got *them* pregnant.

Shadows flickered around Dave's face. "Still," he said, "we're all gonna get married sometime. I've decided to extend our tour so's to include the best honeymoon places in the west."

"Downtown Medicine Hat?" Red perked.

"Marginally better," Dave replied. "We'll visit Lake Louise and Coeur d'Alene."

Lake Louise was obscured by fog; I made a mental note not to get married in September. Detour to Radium Hot Springs for a soak in the sulpherous water; backtrack through Banff and Calgary to Waterton Lakes and across the border into Montana. The United States customs officer waved us on. Dave gunned the motor.

"I've wondered how fast this beast can travel. Montana's got no speed limit." A Buick pulled alongside, challenging: Alex, unnecessarily I thought, splattered its windshield with spittle. The Buick revved. We shot forward. Dave rested the accelerator as we whizzed past Babb, Montana's first hint of habitation; our rival had shrivelled behind. "The trick," Dave imparted, "is to stay in second-gear just a fraction longer than the other guy." Also, I cringed, we'd touched one hundred-thirty miles per hour.

Attracted by Kalispell's trout-shaped advertisement, we unpacked our fishing-gear. Nothing. Sandpoint, in Idaho's panhandle, had a bigger sign; Red reeled in a shoe. We camped outside "Heart of the Woods."

Coeur d'Alene was everything Lake Louise was not. Garish neon and roadside billboards contrasted with Louise's tree-shrouded secretiveness. Impatience versus temperance, separated by the 49th Parallel; I was reminded of St. Joseph's invisible barrier—and that classes were due to resume at university in an unexpectedly short time.

Drive to a hill-crest and glimpse Spokane. "Just to say we've been there," Dave explained. Wheel about and speed to Alberta. Babb again a blur. Flashing lights stop us on the road. A mountie-hatted patrolman brushes snow off his sheepskin jacket.

"Sorry, fellows, the Logan Pass's just been closed."

I hoped Red would conceive a ploy—but I hadn't reckoned with his ingenuity. Focusing on the warden's headgear, he recalled the scout-camp hierarchy. "Major, it is imperative that we be in Edmonton tomorrow."

"Well, now," said the sergeant, "'fore I shut the gate I'll phone ahead that you're comin' on through. Careful though, there's a little blizzard up there."

Plus a white-out. The warden hadn't expected we'd encounter a high mountain snowstorm—the road ahead disappeared, and no guard rails shielded deep canyons to our right. Dave stopped.

"Alex, get the fishing pole and scrape it along the road at arm's-length. If it rubs, we're okay; if it bounces, we're on the shoulder; if it floats, we're angels."

My main concern was not getting home, but registering *on time* —I felt sure, at our slow pace, the barrier at the other end would be locked when we arrived, stalling us until spring.

The car crept. Minimal braking was needed when a figure materialized and approached.

"This's the Canadian gate. Open all your luggage for inspection."

I wished there'd been a Buick beside us.

Dave and I relayed to Edmonton. The eastern sky was a pre-dawn bluish gold when we arrived on 121 Street. I found the front door's key under the geranium pot and wrestled my baggage into the hallway. Glance in the mirror. Haggard stranger. Rummage in the suitcase and locate my electric shaver. Blades whirl. Tiredness vanishes—the razor is clicking, rather than humming, across my cheek. I test it on my chin. No question—the beard has finally arrived.

My younger brother welcomes me at the bathroom door.

"You back?"

"Yeah."

"Too bad, I wanted your room."

"Bug-off. I gotta start university in a couple of hours."

"I've started school already. Grade Ten."

"Congratulations."

"Bill?"

"Yeah?"

"There's a bunch of new teachers."

"So?"

"I dunno how you guys did it but Mr. Sherbanuk's been promoted to St. Joe's." Mickey turned and winked. "Thanks."

21   AUTUMN LEAVES

During registration week's confused mingle, I'd encountered Alex, Alfred, Richard and Robert. Keats had vanished again; Ape was in the seminary; Mert had taken a job. I pressed the doorbell.

"Is Red home?"

"No," his mother replied. "He and Sue flew east yesterday."

"They eloped?"

"Sue's too level-headed for such nonsense. Gordon got a native student scholarship. Sue's in nursing at the same university."

"Where?"

"Sorry, I can't tell even you. Her foster-parents are livid so I have to pretend it was a complete surprise."

"It wasn't?"

She smiled. "Not really. We Blackfoot were born to wander—that's one reason I couldn't stand the reservation. His primordial urge finally caught up; I'm amazed he lasted through high school." The lady hesitated. "Why're you wearing that strange little cap?"

"Have to. U. of A. rules. But just for a couple more days."

"Does it serve any purpose, except to humiliate you?"

"I...don't know, Mrs. Redfeather."

In my bedroom I examined the beanie. Evergreen and gold, the University of Alberta's colors, celebrated Edmonton's river valley splendor in autumn; I hadn't worn similar headgear since my Grade One debut. Perhaps the Students' Union representatives who handed out the hats and name badges were hinting we knew nothing. By the end of frosh week, I guessed why we had been marked.

Senior males converged, like fans paying homage to starlets, around beanied co-eds. Tentative advances on our part were met with aloof rebuffs. I complained to Alfred.

"What's in this for us new guys?"

"A great deal. Conform, and the judges will ignore you on Friday; then the Greeks have a go at you."

"Who?"

"Fraternities. Male in-groups. The frosh cap signifies you're pledge material. They tend, my brother tells me, to approach at your most vulnerable time: standing alone at the Frosh Dance."

"What've they got to offer?"

"They party and aid each other," Alfred sniffed. "Their initiation ceremony usually has something to do with degradation of the naked pledge's body."

"Such as...?"

"Hiring a stripper. Last one to get a hard on's out the door."

"Why'd anybody wanna join?"

"To pass courses with minimum effort. The frats maintain files of old exam questions—profs repeat themselves."

"That'd be handy."

"But also, they have examples of excellent essays, cross-indexed so no two students hand in identical papers."

My step-brother Patrick had been in a fraternity. "They're not all like that." Alfred retracted, "There're several exceptions."

"Who?"

"Look me up Friday evening."

Frosh Court was held in the Education Building auditorium. Several recalcitrants had one arm dyed green and the other yellow, but the general mood conveyed a happy welcome to campus. The bewigged judge stood.

"You may discard your beanies after the dance tonight. Mayor Hawrelak and city council are funding a lavish party. In return, the university has guaranteed there will be *no* traffic-disrupting snake dance downtown." He pounded a gavel. "*That is an order.*"

World War Two officer trainees had honed their marching skills across the Drill Hall's waxed floor; in peacetime, the boards supported examinees, athletes and socializers. Forties music funneled through a narrow doorway and echoed off the hall's high rafters. Spectator seats, accordioned into flatness, formed wood-siding on the east and west walls. North was the orchestra, flanked by a buffet and an ersatz bar where publicans dispensed soft drinks and coffee. I felt uneasy—in a time-warp: the scene resembled dusty Thirties yearbook photos with expressionless couples circling clockwise in the centre, a few venturesome partners at arms-length by the sidelines, and an aimless parade of singles at the periphery.

Pigeons on ceiling beams pooped the slowly moving target below. Alfred was bird watching.

"Fascinating," he observed, his mustache twitching, "how they hit the cleavage almost every time."

An effusive senior pumped my hand. "Hi, I'm Ken," he shouted. "Where'd you graduate from?"

"St. Joe's, in Edmonton."

"Great school. See you around."

"What," I asked Alfred, "was that all about?"

"Steel yourself, old man."

I mocked agony. "Give it to me straight."

"You've just been rejected by a frat."

"Why?"

"Because he found out you're Catholic. Be consoled: they don't admit

Jews or colored races either."

"Unreal!"

"However, true. Were this Alabama rather than Alberta, you'd have to sit at the back of the bus."

"Incredible." I remembered Edwin.

"Believe it. To get around discrimination, the Jews and the Dogans, pardon me, have formed their own frats."

I recalled Pat's picture. "The Delta's?"

"Nope." He cracked his knuckles. "What's being served at the buffet?"

"Hamburgers."

"And it's Friday, right? Catholics can't eat them and Jews can't trust them. Let's get a snake dance going to the mayor's office and show our gratitude for this wonderful evening."

I looked back before entering the High Level Bridge's walkway: news travelled quickly through a four-thousand student campus—the entire town-within-a-city seemed to be moving sinuously toward Edmonton's central core.

At the October examinations, I concluded my marks reflected professorial warnings about tomfoolery. When the Christmas results came, disastrously low, I was stunned. Did the teachers still harbor a grudge?

"Not at all," the student counsellor advised. "They couldn't care less about freshman hijinks. I've seen your I.Q. test and exam results." He leaned forward in his chair. "You're intelligent but not smart. With basic stuff, like physics or chemistry, you did well, but when it came to zoology and botany, you bombed out. Quick! What's the difference between an ant and an elephant?"

"One's big and the other's little."

"Kindergarten response. Think *behind* the question. How does each breathe, eat, see, move and reproduce? Take it further: how would a huge ant be different from a dwarf elephant? Why in fact, is a one-cell plant classed separately from a single-cell animal. *Think.* That's what your professors are trying to awaken in you. It's no good to memorize—that is high-school; *why* is university. He settled back in his chair and closed his eyes. "Why did Shakespeare feel the urge to write Othello?"

"To protest prejudice?"

The eyelids opened slightly. "Welcome to the U. of A."

22   I'M WALKIN'

The second term exam results were better and I had to make a decision: orthodontics or medicine. My dentist squelched the former.

"It's an occupation during good times, but if another depression hits, nobody's gonna pay to have his kid's teeth straightened and you'll be out of a job. Get into a profession where you're not on your feet all day." He sat, stuck a finger in his shoe, and massaged his bunion; I was happy our discussion occurred after he'd metalled my cavities.

The pre-med program meant another year in Arts and Science, plus the prospect of higher registration fees for four years. I phoned Imperial Oil's personnel office.

"Can't take you back," the woman said. "Diefenbaker's government cut all student employment grants."

I began to doubt my Conservative tendency and wondered if old-fashioned Liberal patronage still existed.

"Sure," T.J. exclaimed. "We look after our own. I'll call in a favor or two." He returned from the phone. "Can you learn to drive a truck by the first of May?"

I studied the road rules booklet and passed the written test; a peep-show machine determined I was neither color blind nor lacking in depth perception. An indifferent clerk directed me to the chief examiner.

"You again?" he said.

"Hi there, Mr. School-zone."

"Guys like you take the fun out of my job." We went outside. He sighed and handed me the keys. "Take that beast to the hill, make a U-turn, come back and parallel park it."

"U-turn's illegal up there."

"Like I said...," his voice trailed. "Just park it."

C.W. Boone's warehouse had an eerie similarity to the 95th Street Safeway and the Imperial refinery: all three had beasts in the basement. In the refinery's cavernous rail depot, Mitch wielded a jack and moved freight-cars by himself; at Boone's Jackie did not allow anyone except the dwarf to descend his stairs. Mitch and Jackie were company men: both limped painfully; neither took time off sick. Mitch supervised as we hirelings loaded oil cases and glued them to the railway car's floor—a concession made because his hips wouldn't bend; Jackie had been impressed by our diminutive co-worker's ability to scramble among high-packed crates and retrieve rarely requested orders. (The dwarf delighted in pranks: I made his day when, mechanically stacking boxes off the conveyor belt into my truck, I packed him onto the uppermost tier.)

The maniac, Mitch and Jackie shared a wish to work alone. After my experience with unions, I understood their desire for independence.

I had, as Urban predicted, been laid off when unionized wages increased Safeway's payroll fifty percent. At Imperial, the workers' counter-stategy became evident. The refinery yard-crew was assigned each Monday to a different outfit. Paint, nail, weld, cut, clean, pack or dismantle and the caution was the same: slow down, you're working too fast. I confronted the foreman.

"Look, there's a rhythm to digging this ditch. Let me shovel at my own speed and I'll be done by noon."

"We're digging two ditches."

"So?"

"You dig one this morning and one this afternoon and that other guy's unemployed. Go half-speed and you both work."

"Doesn't seem honest."

"The company's got millions. What's better—some poor guy cashes his pay cheque, buys groceries and eats, or some rich oaf spends his dividends in restaurants and gets fatter?"

I didn't have an answer; the foreman decided to educate me.

"We're taking down the cat-cracker tonight. You're on extra shift. Double pay for overtime."

"Why me?"

"We're allowed a dozen workmen for that job; I've only got eleven."

My task, for eight hours, was to hold a rope attached to a broom wielded by a scrubber in the catalytic tower's central aperture; I could have tied the rope to a guard-rail and gone home—but that was against union rules.

Driving for Boone's I could, within limits, go at my own speed. The police car in the rear-view mirror seemed inordinately interested in my delivery route. I eased across the city boundary at 149th Street to Jasper Place. Haven. He curbed and flicked out his pen and book.

"Don't bother," I said. "Jasper Place belongs to the R.C.M.P."

"The Mounties," he jotted down the license number, "allow us hot pursuit of fugitives."

"I wasn't speeding."

"No, but there was that stop sign at 121st Street you passed."

"Bull! I live there. The only stop signs are for north-south traffic and I was going west."

"North."

I had respected the police until then. The officer's smirk was irritating—he knew who the judge would believe and also that I couldn't afford a day's lost wages spent waiting in court.

Hilda, Boone's chief secretary, was unconcerned. "I'm sure they keep a list of company names. We get a ticket quota each year, same as every other trucker in Edmonton. We write it off against income tax as a business expense."

"Why not fight them?"

Her eyebrows raised. "In Boone's tax bracket, the net cost is half to reduce our property taxes by the full amount the city gets. It's a clever way to have Ottawa subsidize Edmonton. Don't you know how the real world functions?"

I lay in bed that night. My work-mates had been, whether at Safeway, Imperial or Boone's, a singularly dissatisfied lot, each having "a better job" lined up for the future. The refrain recurred in three different environments, so shifting jobs like musical chairs wasn't the answer. Something deeper was involved. Our society, as structured, was fundamentally wrong: cheating and patronage, prejudice and hypocrisy had become accepted behavioral standards; life was a game played by robots pre-programmed to the rules. I flicked on the radio and tuned to Steve Woodman.

Pappy seemed excited. "'Member that Presley fella who sang *Blue Moon of Kentucky*? He's made it big with *Heartbreak Hotel*. Here it is."

The song played. A subliminal chord struck, and faded almost instantly. Pappy was back.

"Fer those of ya that didn't get the message, ol' Pappy'll play an extra tune. Louis Armstrong fans can shut off their radios 'cause this feller's done *Blueberry Hill* like nobody else ever has. Pappy's proud to introduce Fats Domino."

Electric. A different beat. The old song presented with a sudden confidence and strength. Fats was black. Edwin and I had found ourselves in similar circumstances at differing times. I tuned in. The radio radiated raw power, ours for the taking.

Sign off. Silence. The ephemeral feeling struggled to stay, then vanished; I was certain it would return.

23 ALL SHOOK UP

North America buzzed with pre-Christmas excitement in September, 1956: Santa Claus, embodied as Ed Sullivan, descended through rooftop television antennas into the continent's living-rooms with the gift we teens had been awaiting—Elvis Presley in action on camera.

The show was telecast Sunday evening and our parents would be watching; this was a bonus because in the Fifties many topics were taboo and family discussions on matters of substance either never occurred or terminated with platitudes. It seemed important to be with my mother and step-father that night.

I hoped Ed would not impose himself as he had when Les Paul and Mary Ford were guests. The duo introduced taped over-dubbing for guitar and voice; on the final recording, Les had become a strumming quadruplet and Mary a singing twin. The effect couldn't be reproduced for a live stage performance except by playing the original tune and having Les pluck air while Mary lip-synched words. It was demeaning, especially since Sullivan pointedly counted fingers on either hand to signal each overdub's advent.

Ed introduced Elvis, then retreated into the stage's shadow. My relief was transient; the camera swung and showed two front rows occupied by screaming females—obviously planted. But the spotlight revealed more: a youngish bunch in the third row politely applauding and beyond them, just visible in the darkening periphery, a fading circle of frowning adults. Elvis disregarded the audience, looked in close focus straight at us, and slammed into his song.

My parents appeared mystified, I felt satisfied: someone was telling them their comfortable world needed alteration—we weren't going to dance to the old music.

The next day after classes, when the bus reached 108th Street and Jasper Avenue, I didn't transfer and continued on downtown to 104th Street. The Delmar Dance Studio's doorway was sandwiched between the Birks Building to the west and a clothing store: coat collar turned up, I zipped through the entrance.

Eye contact with an olive-skinned girl wearing a sweater, poodle skirt and low-heeled slipper shoes. Her long black ponytail swayed as she approached.

"Hi, I'm Juanita."

Elation, then doubt. "Is that your real name?"

"Yes," she seemed puzzled.

"It's perfect." Wauneita was the honorary society for all co-eds at the U. of A. If I could dance with this Juanita... My apprehension dissolved. "I'm Bill and I wanna learn how to jive."

"No fox-trots, rhumbas or tangos?"

"And no contract."

"You've been there?"

"Yeah. I walked out. How much'll it cost?"

"Can you jitterbug to Glenn Miller's swing beat?"

"No."

"Good. No bad habits to unlearn. Rock and roll's completely different. Twenty dollars for five lessons. That's all it'll take."

"Suppose I need more?"

"You won't," she replied confidently. "I've discovered how to cue in to that music." Juanita selected a record.

"What's that?" I asked, trying to impress her. "*Rock Around the Clock*? *Shake, Rattle and Roll*?"

She tilted her head. "Forget those two. Despite the titles, they're not rock and roll." The turntable clicked. "This is the real stuff." I recognized *Dance With Me Henry*. We went to a full-length wall mirror. She positioned herself three feet away. "Watch what I do. Here's the rock part."

Impossibly intricate and then deceptively simple footwork: a hard hit on the floorboards with toes or heel followed by a soft rocking of the foot back and forth. Right or left didn't matter. She demonstrated every combination and returned to the phonograph.

"My turn?" I was unsure.

"Our turn. We'll do it together."

I was surprised how easy it was to catch the rhythm. "Juanita? What makes rock and roll different?" The record ended and she lifted the needle.

"Those two songs you mentioned are like swing, only with drums instead of brass. They go THUMP-THUMP. Rock goes THUMP-thump. You can recognize it whatever the range."

"The what?"

"Real rock is between fifty-two and sixty hard beats a minute plus the same number of soft ones. It can be slower or faster, but not too far in either direction or it changes."

"Into what?"

"Slow and it becomes Negro blues; super-fast it's the poor white's mountain bluegrass. The middle ground, appropriately enough, is a rock and roll song called *Blueberry Hill*."

"Gonna play it?"

She glanced at her watch. "Next lesson. Practice the rock part, then we'll add the roll."

At the second session we were still separate but she added upper body movement and pivots. At the third, my left palm held her right hand and by the fourth we were easily switching back and forth with the music.

"I think I've got it."

"Maybe," she said. "There's one more lesson. Let's see how you do Friday with *Don't Be Cruel*."

I went to Woodward's record department.

"Sorry," its clerk stated, "the Elvis records are all gone but you're welcome to browse."

Old 78's in slip-sleeve paper covers were relegated, along with their smaller 45 revolution-per-minute counterparts, to boxes in a distant corner. Display rack prominence had been given to cellophane-sealed 33 1/3 discs in thin cardboard sheaths, some having only titles, while others, amazingly, flaunted artwork or a photograph. I examined the seamless cellophane and looked up: Woodward's listening booths bore "Closed" signs—we teens were being told to have faith that modern technology produced flawless records. I flipped through the albums: one caught my eye, and another captured my subconscious.

Juanita had equated music with the color blue so Paul Whiteman and Earl Wild's *Rhapsody In Blue* seemed a logical choice. I instinctively grasped another album; the cover showed an alto saxophone resting against an empty chair—Freddy Gardner was dead but his music still echoed. As I paid the cashier I reflected: despite my penchant for rock and roll, haunting memories from the Forties remained.

Fifth and final lesson. Juanita adjusted the turntable, snapped her fingers rhythmically, and turned. "Ready?" she asked.

I was completely disoriented. "Impossible. I can't dance to that."

"Nonsense." She lifted the needle. "The clue to rock is to feel the beat. Remember 52-60 or 104-120. Take a few seconds and decide which to key in on—the voice, the drums or the bass." She reset the needle and we danced, in harmony.

"You've got it," she said as the record ended. Her hand lingered on my arm.

"Look," she whispered, "I'm getting married next month so don't take this as a come-on."

I stopped and faced her widely-dilated pupils. "What's up, Juanita?"

"Us. I thought me and my boyfriend were the only ones, then you walk through the door and wham, you've got it too."

"Got what?"

"Something. You're in university, right?"

"Yeah."

"Tell me this: how come two strangers can click so suddenly?"

My mind raced to our common denominator. "Dancing?"

"More than that. Why do we have trouble dancing to Glenn Miller and then groove-in when Fats Domino comes on?"

Rapid calculation time. "Fats turned *Blueberry Hill, Jambalaya* and *I'm In the Mood For Love* into rock songs."

"Sure, but why does the rock beat hit us so hard?"

"I dunno, Juanita, but if I ever learn let's get in touch. Where'll you be?"

"Here," she said smiling, "or maybe anywhere."

Disdaining the bus, I wafted home on the cold November wind. Mother shushed my greeting, her attention focused on a television special report.

Hungary was revolting against Soviet rule. A provisional government had been established. The Russians, in retreat, requested a peace meeting with their military adversaries and had, summarily, executed Pal Matyr and the lot. Hungarian politicians were begging, via short-wave radio, for the United States to intervene. World War Three seemed imminent.

I telephoned Alex.

"Ridiculous," he said. "My former countrymen are, unfortunately, idiots. They proclaim Imre Nagy, a known communist, as their leader and expect the U.S. to jump in on their defense? Hopeless. They'd have done better to declare a democracy; then, at least, the Americans would have had an honorable reason to get involved."

"Alex," I cautioned, "both sides've got H-bombs."

"Perhaps," he reflected, "those stay-at-homes aren't as dumb as I thought."

Hungary was pacified, and the world relaxed. President Eisenhower's conservative philosophy had prevailed—change, unless along familiar lines, should be shunned. We'd avoided Armageddon.

But I could not disregard reality: if life was to continue, the future had to be plotted—in concert with profound alterations in my immediate U. of A. world, caused by John Chappel.

Our Students' Union president had issued decrees and ultimatums: the Frats must integrate, the teaching staff must abolish automatic percentage class failure, and all students, regardless of anything except ability, should have access to quota-restricted faculties. Revolutionary. Because they came from an American, the orders were initially reviled by administration. Then John shrewdly marshalled his forces: a hundred to one against every defined target resulted in capitulation. Individual merit in each case won the day. I felt at ease talking with Chappel in the Tuck Shop: our oratorical lion was a dialectical lamb. Nothing, he insisted, counted as much as effort: expend it, and you'll be rewarded. A truly radical concept for the Fifties.

Assured, via Alex, that the world would not self-destruct, and through John that I'd have an even chance at entering the Faculty of Medicine, I looked further to the future and contemplated serious dating. Richard and Robert were no help when I interrupted their heated conversation in "The

Hot Calf."

The U. of A.'s hot cafeteria provided us with surprisingly edible food. The building achieved its nickname from a picture of a sweating heifer—though we all knew the implication really referred to the nylon seams extending like fuses from our co-eds' lower legs upward to the forbidden zone. It was a popular place to gather.

I set down my tray; Robert was livid. "My frat's got direct connections to that sorority."

"Beware," Richard's pink face replied, "those girls are a den of venomous lesbians."

"Five bucks," Robert snarled, "says I'll get one of them pregnant by Easter."

Alfred joined us. "Too late, old chap. I'll have the entire bunch missing their periods by Christmas."

Absurd, yet somehow believable. I couldn't resist asking.

"Give us your secret, Alfred."

"Gamesmanship, dear boy," he muttered. "It is incumbent upon you to reduce any advantage claimed by the other side. He who is not one-up is, by definition, one-down."

"How about everybody being equal?"

"Two guys take one girl to a movie?"

"I see what you mean."

The competition was on. Grade-school crushes and high-school infatuations meant nothing: the crunch had come—find a mate or be celibate forever.

The U. of A. lent itself to this singular pursuit; as the only university in the province, its female co-eds were conveniently distanced from their families. St. Joseph's College assumed the parental role for Catholics—Brother Luke and staff lectured on how science complemented religion: the more we learned about our world and universe, the less we would believe they hadn't been planned. At the same time Newman Club members were organizing dances: since we sinners had chosen not to enter seminaries or convents, a site would be provided for us to meet, with the idea, I surmised, that we'd eventually marry and produce umpteen purer souls.

I resented the Newman Club's temerity. Why should they assume Catholics would voluntarily attend their Friday night tea-party, undoubtedly featuring boys along one wall and girls against the other? I hipped my textbooks and started upstairs. T.J. met me on the landing.

"Park your notes and," he tossed the car keys, "vanish. The big canasta tournament's tonight and we winners can get noisy. You won't be able to concentrate."

I couldn't study at the university's Rutherford Library—on Fridays the place was deserted and I'd feel oddly alone. Okay, drift with the tide; check out the Newman matrimonial agency.

The auditorium rocked with the liveliest music I had ever heard on campus. Couples were either dancing or supporting each other breathlessly on the sidelines. The song ended, to loud applause, and more music erupted as everyone changed partners. Amidst the mayhem I saw a familiar face. She'd poured Bernie Faloney that fateful cup of coffee. The St. Mary's grad was dancing in time to the rhythm: her partner was not. He collapsed against the wall while she looked around for a new conquest.

Fear is strong, but pheromones are stronger. Poodle-cut, flare skirt, about five-foot four with a devastating smile, plus my rival gasping on the bench—obviously one-down. Gamesmanship time.

"Hi, Calgary. Love your accent."

Her surprised protest was obscured by the next rock song's drum and guitar beat. My lips moved silently under the din. We shrugged, accepted the inevitable and swung into action. She was like Juanita, yet different: it wasn't teacher and pupil, but rather equals interacting. We clicked. Then Catholicity's coyness intervened. I got her phone number only after confiding that Elizabeth and Irene, her back-home neighborhood friends, were my cousins.

The upstairs lights were on at home. I leaned against the bedroom doorway. Mother marked her book.

"Who won?" I asked.

"No matter," she answered characteristically. I concluded she and T.J. had wiped out the opposition. "Sit down and tell me about her."

My knees became greasy. "How did you...?"

Her eyes moistened. "It's not what I wanted. I've prayed you'd become a priest."

"Sure, but how'd you know I met someone."

"Because you look exactly as I felt on the night I met your father."

24   HONEYCOMB

Our attitude on campus changed in 1956. Like guerrilla bands merging into a unified army, the first generation of the atomic age found a rallying point: the new music, *our* music, burgeoned—and each week the excitement increased. It was as if the student population had become an enormous radio, each part attuned to the invisible airwaves.

Fats fattened his repertoire with *Ain't That A Shame*. Sound-alikes Gene Vincent and Ivory Joe Hunter countered by recording *Be Bop A Lula* and *Since I Met You Baby*. Frankie Lyman's *Why Do Fools Fall In Love* struck a respondent chord among us. Little Richard's *Rip It Up*, *Tutti Fruitti* and *Lucille* added to the fun. But Presley was the colossus on our radio frequencies—from the slow *Love Me Tender* to an almost-bluegrass *Hound Dog*. He spanned the rock spectrum, abetted by female co-creators. Kay Starr taunted our elders when she sang the *Rock And Roll Waltz*, then smashed all hypocrisy with *Bonaparte's Retreat* . Gogi Grant more gently hinted that a turning point had come in *The Wayward Wind*. We rocked, and so did the establishment's foundation.

Nothing was sacrosanct. Politics were parodied by Pogo Possum. Stan Freberg savaged TV, nursery rhymes and, with his memorable *Elderly Man River*, censorship in all its guises. *Mad Magazine* mocked the hitherto serious, and *Playboy*—in contrast to the geographic journals—subliminally implied the bare-breasted woman who yearned for spiritual enlightenment while looking straight at the camera was really the girl-next-door daring us. Pretenses vanished: both male and female groins were gurgling.

We could hardly contain ourselves when the Archbishop, cloaked and mitred, delivered a sombre sermon on rock and roll—his ornate shepherd's crook resembled a microphone.

Nor were our teachers spared. When Dr. Hocking announced he intended to fail one-third of the sixty-member entomology class, twenty students stood and walked out. I raised my hand (having learned about the birds in zoology, I was still curious about bees). "Does this mean the rest of us have passed?"

"It would appear so," came the bemused reply.

Alex took on Brother Andrew, whose preoccupation was to interpret the Bible literally.

"You'd better believe it," Andy warned. "If the Bible said the dog's tail wagged then that's the truth: think any different and you're damned. God said to Moses, 'Thou shalt not have strange gods before Me.' Anyone care to differ?"

Alex coughed. "I doubt that Moses understood English."

Alfred challenged the geology instructor: asked to make a relief map showing land elevations in a square-mile area, he drew a quadrangle, left it blank, and gave the coordinates for the northeast corner's lake surface. Full marks for guts.

And so it went. Prelates, politicians and professors tried to fight back: but prayer seemed less important than penicillin for warding off disease—plus Salk's polio vaccine had made our crowding together quite safe. We laughed when Ottawa warned that loud rock music could obscure air raid siren warnings: we aced the university's examinations, disdaining terror at mid-term or cringing at Christmas so better to concentrate on real studying of the Students' Union telephone directory.

Our dating options were limited. Since bowling, the choral society and quiet walks on campus didn't count, the choice narrowed to either a dance at the Drill Hall followed by illicit beer in frat houses, or a movie downtown with a well-timed rush afterward to the Purple Lantern's food. Anyone caught in the theatre when the first bars of *God Save The Queen* sounded stood and sang good-bye to any chance of getting a table at the Chinese restaurant. The format was stereotyped and too hectic; something different was in order. An article in *The Edmonton Journal* perked my interest.

"The hottest action in town," a columnist wrote, "is at Omar's Oasis on 124th Street."

I tried to call Dody at Pembina Hall.

"She's gone to a show," the prefect apologized.

I reassured myself that the competition lacked imagination; the next day I dialled earlier. Dody came on the line. She'd never heard of Omar's but found the novelty appealing.

"Do they serve Middle Eastern dishes? How spicy are they?"

"The hottest in town," I bluffed. "Saturday at eight?"

"Okay." She paused. "Will this be a double-date?"

"No, and with good reason." I recounted the drive-in fiasco with Red, Sue, and Margie. "Good enough?"

"Marginal. See you Saturday."

T.J. acknowledged that I'd installed our home's storm windows without being asked and relinquished his car. I got it washed and had my charcoal-grey suit drycleaned. The reservation at Omar's was reconfirmed. Nothing would be left to chance on *this* date.

I guided Dody's elbow in her descent of Pembina's perilous front steps and closed the Pontiac's door *after* she'd swept her calf-length plaid skirt into the car's interior. The motor ignited with my key's first turn and the gears didn't grind. So far so good. We glided to a smooth stop at an intersection. Dody broke the silence.

"Does talking interfere with your concentration?"

I felt foolish. "No, but thanks for asking. Tell me how you wound up here in Edmonton."

"Not before *you* 'fess up how you knew I was from Calgary."

"You're famous for starting the St. Mary's food fight. Name and picture in all the papers..."

"You were there *that* night? I've suppressed it, but I know it didn't hit the news. Come on."

I looked at her and feigned shock. She laughed and waved my gaze back to the road. We chatted. I relaxed: nothing could go wrong. She was taking the B.Sc. program in nursing—a four-year course. During the second year, in addition to classes, there would be eight-hour shifts on the hospital wards—at a monthly salary of twelve dollars and fifty cents.

Brake lights were blinking on the High Level Bridge. We eased forward and came upon the congestion's cause: two males, naked, running side-by-side on the pedway, their fraternity's car keeping pace. I half-expected Dody to get out, slam the door and storm home but instead she snuggled closer. Was she asking protection from the wanton or thanking me for the turn-on? I concentrated, found a gap and accelerated the car north to Jasper Avenue. We hard-wheeled west to 124th Street and eased into Omar's parking lot. A patron, emptying his bladder, turned full-frontally to face our headlights. Dody spoke first.

"How much," she asked, "are you paying these guys?"

I mumbled a mortified disclaimer and we scurried under Omar's palm-tree and sand dunes sign, its neon buzzing defiantly against the icy November wind. An animated crowd filled the warm doorway. A decidedly greasy little man, in a wrinkled tuxedo, was directing traffic.

"Downstairs. Pleased to see you again. Downstairs. Welcome once more. Watch your step." He faced us. "Yes?"

"Two, for dinner."

He seemed startled. "You want to eat?"

"Yes."

We followed him to an isolated table. The dining room was deserted. We sat, watching a stream of patrons descend to the lower level. A waiter eventually appeared and poured two unrequested cups of coffee. He stood as we perused the menu, then spoke.

"Stove's down. I can fetch a cheese sandwich if ya want."

My indignant response was cut short by whistles. Police whistles. The raiding force zeroed in downstairs. Customers in handcuffs ascended followed by officers heaving betting wheels and balancing stacks of chips. Confusion. Our waiter reappeared.

"We're closed. Coffee's on the house."

When we bade goodnight, I was certain she'd never date me again.

"Uh, Dody, about this evening..."

She stopped me and pecked my cheek before entering Pembina's glassed-in doorway. "Wouldn't have missed it for the world."

Okay. One-up. But how to top it? I took a chance and phoned an ancient number. He answered, in his usual manner.

"This is Keats. You are permitted to speak."

"Cut the crap, Dave. We've got an emergency."

He listened and offered a solution. "Call her up," he said, "and suggest Club Anton for Friday."

I'd never heard of it. "You sure?"

"Positive. To cement the deal, tell her you'll be double-dating with us."

"You going steady?"

"She thinks so," he answered enigmatically. "We'll pick you up at seven."

I sensed Dody's nervousness: neither of us knew what Keats had planned. His Packard swung off 101st Street onto a dimly-lit 106th Avenue. A seedy, run-down area surrounded us. One bare light-bulb outlined Anton's hand-lettered sign. I didn't want to move.

Dave opened the passenger door. "Come on, you two, we're missing the fun." He pointed: his date had already reached Anton's entrance. We followed.

Our path led down a dark stairwell to a murky cloak-room. We doffed our coats, noting each hook's location, and tracked along the short hallway to an auditorium guarded by a hostess. Keats paid her two dollars, the admission fee for a quartet. The place was almost full but we found a table and ordered Coke and doughnuts—the only fare available. The stage lights switched on and a group carrying instruments appeared: I saw a trumpet, trombone, clarinet, and banjo. Two other musicians positioned themselves by the drums and piano. The audience, until now quiet, erupted into wild applause when a hefty female vocalist appeared. The trumpeter tipped his straw-boater backward, pulsed an arm, and the music started. I looked at Dody the instant she looked at me. We'd discovered the excitement of Edmonton's best-kept secret—The Tailgate Jazz Band.

Dixieland was rock and roll's cousin. There was no difficulty adjusting to the beat when dancing: we found ourselves standing to acclaim a second encore at the evening's end.

"Dating you," Dody remarked outside Pembina, "is certainly different."

I took the challenge: our next trip was to Chic's Bar-B-Q on the Calgary Trail. The unassuming little shack had great food, a dance floor and an up-to-date juke-box. Some songs, by mutual agreement, we sat out; others impelled us to participate and experience their unrestrained vitality.

"Strange," Dody said, drawing me closer.

"How so?"

"That two people from different cities all of a sudden find each other."

25 THAT'LL BE THE DAY

"Steven," Martha's quavering tone implored, "you *must* stop him. He awakened Teeny with Mr. Presley's *All Shook Up* and now he'll keep the child wall-eyed with that demonstration record he's clutching."

"Now, now," Steve cautioned. "Maybe it's a lullaby."

Pappy wheezed in anticipation. "Lemme play it."

"Steven, I'm warning you..."

The announcer stretched away from the microphone, his distant voice reading a label. "Says here the singer's Buddy Holly."

Martha was mollified. "I went to school with a boy named Buddy. Quietest fellow in the class."

"This," replied Pappy, "is prob'ly his great-grandson."

Although the June evening was hot, I shivered: Holly's rock beat struck dead-centre; several seconds of silence at the song's end told me Steve was also impressed. Teeny spoke.

"That woke me up even more, Uncle Stevie."

"Steven, I *insist* you play something quiet."

The opening bars sounded. *Moonlight Bay.* Steve sang a duet with Doris Day, and complemented her perfectly. The record ended with Teeny snoring.

"Goodnight," Steve whispered.

I switched off the radio and wished Dody had shared the moments—she'd returned home to Calgary when university ended in April.

I had busied my weekdays working as a groundskeeper at the Country Club golf course, spending Saturdays in Safeway. Sunday was the time for maintenance work around house and yard. The evenings were incredibly lonely.

The episode began with a superficially innocuous, but very odd, telephone call. Mother Igneous was on the line; I hadn't spoken with her since Grade Nine, five years before. She was, as usual, blunt.

"The high school prom is next week and one of my convent girls doesn't have an escort. Will you accompany her to the dance?"

A St. Joe's grad would know all the boys in that school. Nobody had asked her. Perhaps she was plain, or even downright ugly, but it didn't matter—she was dateless for grad night and I sympathized with her situation.

"Sure. What time?" I was direct-dating the caller.

"Seven-thirty would be fine," she replied coyly, as if stirring long-lost memories. Reality returned when she added, "A corsage would be appropriate." The nuns nevèr left anything to chance.

What to wear? Each pimple-faced male grad would be adorned in a charcoal grey suit with pink shirt and handkerchief, his tie held down by a broad yellow bar. Those guys had rejected my date and she needed to be one-up. Why not? I selected grey slacks and a U. of A. blazer with its gold-embossed varsity crest on the jacket pocket. My neophyte required a lesson: facing a barrier, you should vault beyond it rather than try to bulldoze through.

Convents have weird doorbells: press them, there's silence, and a nun appears before your finger's left the buzzer. Mother Igneous snatched the corsage box, obviously concerned carnal lusts would be aroused should the flowers be pinned in my presence. I waited in the parlor. Starch rustled; Mother Igneous waved her hand.

"Please meet," she said, her lips scarcely moving, "Leda." Her manner said it all: since there was no St. Leda, this girl wasn't Catholic.

Leda was not on the ugly edge of plain—she was on the gorgeous side of beautiful.

"I am," she explained in the car, "an inmate in that prison. My parents couldn't handle me so they got the nuns in on the job."

"Nobody asked you to the dance?"

"Lots of guys said they'd call, but the phone was censored."

"Your name's ...Leda?"

"Yeah. Daddy loves Greek mythology." She surveyed me. "Guess I'm destined to date turkeys."

Her party was at the Trocadero Ballroom. Leda's interest was piqued when I extracted a twenty-six-ounce booze bottle from the glove compartment. She was further impressed when I slid the hooch into one of the Troc's hollow table legs. In the Fifties, liquor consumption was restricted to homes, licensed hotel beer rooms, and wherever you could get away with it. Wine with meals was unknown, all restaurants being officially dry. The Troc had a pat excuse: they'd been offered an irresistible deal on furnishings and the secret compartments totally escaped management's notice.

Speeches completed, a band occupied front stage. Music. I raised my eyebrows, Leda reluctantly stood. Marathon rock. She was gasping when the final notes pounded down.

"You are," she said, "not as bad as I feared."

"And you, I suspect, are not as good as the nuns would like."

"I'm hot." She doffed her demure bolero jacket, revealing shoulders and arms. Mother Igneous would not have approved.

Next number. Leda seemed irritated.

"These damn straps are cutting into my shoulder. Unsnap them at the back."

I hesitated. "How's your dress gonna stay up?"

She guided my hand from her rigid waist up behind to a similarly-braced thorax. "The secret's in the corset; it braces up my boobs. Don't worry."

I rapidly recalled mail-order catalogue pictures of torso-armored females. "How do you breathe?"

She guided my hand lower to softer territory. "The bottom half's missing."

I looked at her crossed legs and attempted sophisticated understanding. "Those long garters must be a problem."

"I cut them off."

"How do your stockings stay up?"

"The nuns don't know I smuggled in a garter belt."

More music. Leda's face was flushed.

"You okay?"

She excused herself. "Need a bit more breathing room." On her return, she stuffed something into my blazer's unflapped pocket.

"My panties. Let's dance."

The definite impresssion of being seduced was reinforced when, during slow songs, her thighs tried to determine whether I'd grown a third leg. The situation was obvious: Mother Igneous trusted me to keep this nymph under control.

From the dance we went to a house party and then to a pre-dawn breakfast at another home. I discarded my empty liquor bottle beside the porch. Maybe, with food, she'd come to her senses. No chance—the bacon and eggs were washed down with champagne. Leda was decidedly tiddly when we collapsed in the car. I drove south on 109th Street and approached Jasper Avenue; one block right and two south and she'd be home.

"Turn left," Leda ordered.

"East?"

"School's over; I'm checked out. Take me to the MacDonald."

The sky had turned from black to blue. Taller buildings reflected sunlight. I parked in front of the hotel. The MacDonald was a CNR establishment and someone was getting railroaded.

We entered the lobby and were greeted by a leering night bellhop. Leda pushed the fifth floor elevator button and extracted a key from her tiny, sequined party-purse. Walk down the corridor and pause at 522.

"Come on in and meet my parents."

"Parents?"

"Yeah, they're driving me home."

"Leda, its five o'clock in the morning."

"They won't mind."

Hesitation. She was from Mundare, an almost-suburb of Edmonton. And her parents hadn't been at the graduation dinner. There were two, possibly three, scenarios:

her parents were there, and would be most grouchy on being awakened...

the room was vacant, and any bed, at this late hour, was extremely tempting; or, pre-dawn paranoia prevailed...

Mother Igneous would be ensconced in the room ready to denounce the lecher.

I needed time. "Leda, I think the keys are in the car."

The bellhop smirked. "Struck out, eh, sport?"

I approached the short man. His arms assumed a defensive posture. I took out my wallet. "Will five bucks keep you quiet?"

The hands dropped. "Guaranteed."

I extracted the panties. "Get the maid to use her pass-key and toss these in the bathroom as soon as she comes on shift."

My adversary's eyes widened. "Jeez, boss, you work fast." He took the fiver. "Consider it done."

A good investment—better than explaining to her father, if present, how his daughter's underclothes had come into my possession.

26 THE MAGIC TOUCH

In autumn, the mountains echo when rams butt heads together. Elk bellow. Deer risk fracturing fragile hind limbs. Squirrels chatter and pair-up for hibernation. Fall is the rutting season: whether by accident or subconscious design, it corresponds with the time students return to school.

Alfred stroked his mustache and inspected the female frosh clustered around a nearby table. "Little lambs waiting to be shorn."

"Don't underestimate." My escape from the hotel remained a vivid memory. "Some of them want their wool back."

"Please elucidate."

"They're after your socks."

"Even better, old chap."

Alex joined us. He too had chosen the Hot Calf's newest menu addition—pizza pie. "It looks different from what I had in Italy."

Essential ingredients had been obtained but our chefs, not bothering to translate the recipe's text, assembled the offering in a singularly peculiar order. Alex did the dissection.

"Bread dough. They got that right." His fork tapped along the cut edge. "Next we have sliced olives and," the fork rose, "an inch of hamburger. The centimeter of cheese on top, substituted for mashed potatoes, tells me they think this is the Mediterranean equivalent to shepherd's pie."

Tentative bites turned into a ravenous demolition. We went back for seconds. Alfred toyed with the crust edge on his plate.

"We were lucky to get into med school."

"Yeah," I said. "It sank in at registration this morning."

Alex disagreed. "I heard there were only fifty-nine applications. A fellow from Commerce told me Dean Scott phoned and got him to change faculties so the quota would be filled."

"You mean," I hunched forward to reduce eavesdropping, "we *all* got accepted?"

"Every last man."

Plus five women who entered the pantisocracy when our group gathered for the Dean's welcoming address. It didn't seem odd that the class was all-white: students from a different race were uncommon, if not rare, on campus in 1957. My attention focused on the age differential among us. An appraisal was necessary: our faculty retained the one-third-shall-fail rule.

We were mostly twenty, or about six months on either side. A younger bunch had obviously skipped a grade or two; they merited watching.

Others, older, I recognized from graduate photos in the Evergreen and Gold year-books; perhaps, having taken three terms to decide on a career in medicine, they weren't cut-throat competitors.

Last, I noted a trio who appeared to have at least fifteen years more worldly experience than the rest. One rejuvenated herself by mimicking our youthful zeal. The second, alert to campus tricks, imparted his wisdom with tips on point-form writing and subtle bluffing through the dreaded essay and oral examinations. Then there was Tony, a Crowsnest Pass coal miner who'd decided on a job where the sun shone. Initially reserved, he scanned the terrain and stayed. No one suspected that within two months Tony would rise up to assume class leadership.

"Medicine," the Dean hummed, "is built upon tradition and respect. We learn from the past so better to anticipate the future. You must realize your teachers have been along paths you've never travelled, and your patients—should you ever get that far—will rely upon *your* guidance. Respect both: the former for the time they have spent and the latter for the trust they place in you. Until this century, life tended to be brutal and short. Modern advances have made the biblical three score years and ten possible: your job will be to assure *that* existence is comfortable and productive. The guiding principle is to do no harm. At times, diseases will defeat your efforts and the patients' resolve. Accept it. No one thanks you if aggressive treatment results in a bed-ridden state for three months when the alternative was thirty functional days at home or work. You will not, over the next four years, be imbued with divine healing powers so remember: the most important task is to aid and not hinder the human body's remarkable resiliency. Eventually, of course, death is inevitable for all of us and you will soon encounter people who have succumbed. Dr. Thompson?"

My fleeting mental picture of a corpse being wheeled in was dispelled when "Jungle Jim" stood. We'd all taken zoology and dissected worms, frogs, turtles and rats. But gross anatomy was different—people, like us, had to be carved open. Dr. Thompson spelled his name and chalked a text-book list on the blackboard: other professors taking his cue did the same—Dean Scott was a hard act to follow.

At home in my room I flipped through the anatomy book and back-leafed to a picture that evoked dizziness and nausea. The man's head was in restful repose, right eyelids together, lips in peaceful neutrality: the left side, in contrast, showed bare muscles and a round, staring globe that leapt from the page. My vertiginous gaze made the skinless left face tremble. I shut the book lest its apparition begin speaking what it surely would ask: did I have the guts to continue this course?

Entering the anatomy room I was relieved to see the cadavers' heads tightly gauzed. A right upper limb was exposed for dissection—bad enough, but tolerable. Foursomes assigned to each stretcher shuffled and feigned bravado, not daring to touch the mottled bodies. Dr. Rawlinson understood our reluctance.

"The key," he said, "is to realize there's a distance between you and the patient. Great doctors reduce the gap to a fractional space, but it's still present. Here, imagine you're wearing rubber gloves so if *his* skin's cut *you* don't feel like bleeding. Put an invisible shell around yourselves. When patients come to see you it's essential to understand but fatal to identify with them. You must be concerned, but dispassionate, observers. Therein exists sanity." He adjusted his glasses. "These people willed their bodies to science: don't disappoint their souls."

We lost five classmates that day and a sixth—the commerce student—announced at week's end he felt more comfortable with numerical figures. An additional four quit after the October mid-term examinations—which were highlighted by Jungle Jim's oral quiz on anatomical specimens. Thompson's pride was a muscle supplied by overlapping nerves—a supposedly unique combination. He shook his head while I muddled through the differential diagnosis. Tony was next: I lingered near the doorway.

"What's this?" Jim inquired.

"A goddam hunk of meat on a string."

"You misunderstand. The muscle is..."

"Crap. Nobody walks into an emergency department swinging it like bait and saying, 'Please put this back where it belongs.'"

"But..."

Tony towered. "Gimme something fair or get ready to eat that thing."

He got the alternate specimen. So much for tradition and respect.

We envied Tony's courage—a crack had appeared in the faculty's castle wall. Medicine seemed to be a series of steep steps, locked doorways and drawbridges. The outer rampart was ominous: information overload, with thick textbooks requiring literal memorization. Next came an ascent through spot quizzes structured cleverly to weed out the lazy and faint-hearted. If we found the key for unlocking major tests, and persisted through eighteen-hour days, permission would be granted to cross a moat into second year. But first we could expect boiling-oil baths on the Christmas and final examinations.

The class was running scared and simultaneously reached the same conclusion: we needed one night in a meeting *cum* party for marshalling our forces to consolidate the counter-attack. Ten of us had fallen: they were, in retrospect, easy targets. Joe Martin was safe: on any given exam he was twenty percent above the class average. That left forty-nine, ten destined for elimination—all within our narrowly-based grade point cluster.

We met at the Delta Upsilon House on Saskatchewan Drive and followed the music down an oak staircase to the party room. Admission was twelve beers or two dollars, the latter to accommodate our Mormons and other teetotallers who'd choose pop and peanuts over booze and pretzels. Songs blared from the ceiling loudspeaker. Brewery products were stacked near the doorway. Random clusters of students engaged in small talk. The evening had no focus until Tony clinked two bottles together.

"I challenge anyone to match me." He set the empties on the mantle-piece and uncapped a third.

I gave up after four. Some managed ten. The closest competitor hit twenty-two by midnight, while Tony calmly added the thirtieth "dead soldier" to his collection. He was upright and clear-eyed. He spoke.

"Those bastards are trying to grind us down. I've been through too much to let them beat me. I ain't gonna be de-testiculated and I guess our women don't wanna be oophorectomized. We've gotta choice: either put on their straight-jacket or bust free. I dunno about the rest of you guys but I'm pissed off with the games they're playing."

We nodded agreement.

"I didn't hear you," said Tony, cupping his ear. "Worried someone might be listening?"

Tony couldn't have timed it better: at that moment our ceiling played *The Worried Man Song* and the class cheered its new leader.

Alfred slid his shoulder up the wall. "Are you," he shouted, "a prophet or a general?"

"Neither goddamn one, you English twit. Don'tcha know a bulldozer blade when you see it? We're gonna grind them down. Who's with me?"

We roared again.

"I'm gonna shake every hand that's here tonight again in 1961."

We believed him.

Tony was our graduating year's class president.

27 HEART OF MY HEART

Steve's coterie expanded as Edmonton's huge younger population twirled dashboard dials or discretely bade TV-mesmerized parents goodnight before tuning bedroom radios on CKUA to get the *real* news.

Steve never disappointed us. Acquiring in some mysterious way every significant American pre-release, he introduced a landmark: Buddy Holly's *Peggy Sue*. Super-fast music, but with lyrics sung in the exact rock beat range Juanita had described; the rhythm and voice combination radiated energy. Presley's *Teddy Bear* had the same explosive effect. Buddy Knox added *Party Doll*. Then came the Everly Brothers' *Wake Up Little Susie*, about a couple who'd fallen asleep at a drive-in movie. The older generation was scandalized and demanded censorship. Steve complied by playing Susie with its offending words intact and each mention of parents in the song dead-aired: the result was hilarious.

We also laughed when a politician attempted to equate Sputnik's launch in October, 1957, with a world-wide brainwashing plot: the Soviet satellite's beep-beep was hopelessly out of sync with the rock rhythm.

Pastors railed, teachers warned and parents cautioned: our music was threatening society's structure. I recalled what Dean Scott had said. If tradition and respect were keystones in the hierarchy, the system as they knew it was indeed troubled. To paraphrase Pogo, the enemy was them.

Reading to a class word-by-word from books we'd all purchased was not teaching. Nor did a dissertation on the professor's current obscure research project seem relevant. Our restlessness grew when we realized Medicine, the most archaic faculty, regarded century-old customs and ideas as sacrosanct. Imitating ancient diviners, we apprentices had to discern function from intertwining muscles, blood vessels and nerves, and relate the tangle to as-yet undescribed injury and disease. We had a glimmer of hope about our psychiatry lecturer who must have dealt with living people. He introduced himself as a doctrinaire Freudian and began the talk. Hope changed to angry glances. Did this guy *really* believe monkeys feared snakes because the latter were phallic symbols? He did. We weren't convinced.

The genetics professor gave breathless accounts relating fetal growth to malformed offspring as if such were the norm. I looked around the class and recalled my childhood acquaintances: while none of us was perfect, we were the majority. One could only conclude she was a secular plant from some convent giving celibacy its final sales-pitch.

The faculty's attitude toward us was evident the day a physiology instructor, obviously annoyed at having to leave the department's Christmas party, emptied his bladder in the classroom sink before commencing a slurred dissertation. Tony summed our feelings.

"Piss on *them*," he said.

Resentment didn't help. While our marks for physiology labs were spectacular—Alex had discovered how to cook results for muscle-nerve tracings on smoked drums—the written test was a calamity. Anatomy chose to quiz us on the fine print and footnotes in Gray's text, assuming we'd spent scarce time cross-referencing in the library. Biochemistry was fair, only because new methods of sugar, fat and protein metabolism hadn't yet been postulated, so our notes held firm on recitation. Conversely, genetics was reeling from Watson and Crick's DNA discovery: we exploited the staff's confusion by citing *Time* magazine. And in passing we humored the Freudian. But, together, December was disaster month when the results were posted.

In retrospect, the mid-term's intense interrogations had a purpose—to weed out the uncommitted.

After Christmas the survivors were rewarded with pure gold: Ralph Shaner and Sam Hanson imparted knowledge on, respectively, neuroanatomy and embryology.

Dr. Shaner shuffled into the amphitheatre. Rumples on his clothes matched wrinkles on his face. He paused, struck a wood match, puffed his pipe to life, and gazed across our doubting faces.

"I know how you feel. Somebody took a movie film, cut it up, shuffled the pieces and thrust a single frame forward asking you to reconstruct the plot."

Exactly. We murmured agreement.

"I'm a rebel," he continued. "I don't subscribe to unnecessary confusion." He selected a chalk stick. "The nervous system is complex in structure but simple in function. Allow me," he bowed, "to show you how it works."

A brilliant exposition. Isolated data interlocked. We shared understanding with contagious enthusiasm. I jotted his final remarks, set down my pen, and stood. The class was already upright and applauding.

I didn't think Shaner's lectures could be surpassed. They weren't, until mid-way through the second term.

Dr. Hanson disdained the authoritative lab coat. His business suit flowed comfortably as he settled on the classroom's four-legged tall stool.

"I'm a pathologist at the Edmonton General Hospital across the river. It's a bit of a mystery why they parachuted me in, but my job's to tell you where *your* heart came from. We'll begin with how some embryonic cells decide to pump blood rather than think, and we'll discuss how their best intentions are thwarted if developmental cues are missed."

Sam had us. He personalized medicine by lucidly telling the story of why *we* hadn't died in the womb or succumbed as newborns.

"You're here," he said, "through an extraordinary combination of luck and chance. It's not surprising things go wrong: rather, it's amazing how often the whole system turns out normally."

Dr. Hanson's lectures instilled immense confidence—truth was easy to understand, especially when a *rondeau* was established with Dr. Shaner's discussions: the brain worked the heart and the heart nourished the brain.

Sam concluded his series. "The primordial heart rate is one hundred-twenty beats per minute. There is a decrease over the next year to one-hundred four as an infant distances itself from the womb and asserts independence by standing and walking. The brain, in effect, takes over, but somehow I feel the original heartbeat lingers on somewhere to reassure us, now and then, that we're still alive."

I sat, stunned, the back of my scalp intolerably irritated. The butterfly left when I unpocketed a coin, hurried to the pay phone, and dialed Delmar.

She didn't work there any more.

28 ONE NIGHT

We all agreed the law was silly but it existed nonetheless. In the Fifties no one, regardless of military service, marriage or achievements in professional and business careers, reached official adult status before age twenty-one. The legal reality was generally disregarded by merchants and government—I'd worked part-time and filed income tax returns since age fourteen—but there was one major exception: Alberta's Liquor Control Board. My mandatory coming-of-age party required tacit legislative approval. The clerk was surprisingly helpful in 1958.

"I'll hold the beer keg for you when our four o'clock shipment comes in. Make the rest of your purchases earlier in the day and don't worry. August 29th, right?"

I confirmed the date.

"You'll need a spout-dispenser. That'll be an extra deposit."

I proffered money and the clerk swept it into the till. He paused. "Got enough for everything else?" The cash register stayed open. "If you don't, hold off on this rental fee. We can sometimes bend the rules."

In Edmonton, "everything else" entailed patronizing four other establishments: The Palace of Sweets for salted and caramel popcorn; the Nut House to obtain assorted munchies; National Bakery, so hamburgers could be held comfortably; and Sid's Butcher Shop—the latter choice varied with each neighborhood. One of my jobs had been to deliver on bicycle for Sid's—and for Carrington's Drug Store next door. Sid supplied Burger King: the drive-in restaurant never ordered antacids.

"Everything's looked after," I assured the clerk.

Friday arrived. I tapped the alarm clock button and lay back in bed. My parents could now, legally, kick me out of their house. Likely? No. T.J., in addition to his diabetes, had been afflicted with cancer: my mother could soon be a widow again. But suppose Mother forgot to take her blood pressure pills and had a stroke; would T.J. maintain the family? Yes, I reasoned, because among the remaining trio, only Mickey and I knew how to cook—we each had our specialties—and T.J. would starve without us. Coffee time. I went downstairs, brewed a cup, and returned to bed. What had I *learned* in the past twenty-one years? Laval had distinguished education from training. Was I cued, like Clancy, to respond to external stimuli or could I *think*, in the manner of Ralph Shaner and Sam Hanson? I didn't know for certain, but parental guidance afforded some assurance: I'd been taught equanimity, resourcefulness and decisiveness—with all the traits reinforced in a single evening. Why Florence and T.J. were such formidable opponents had become apparent during one memorable bridge game.

The cards were sitting well and Mother was pleased. "Go with the tide," she murmured, before bidding and bringing home a game contract. Subtly, the momentum turned and their opponents took advantage. Mother rose, and in a scarcely audible voice said, "I'm restless." She circled her chair and the adversary distractedly gave his cards an *extra* shuffle. Game contract again. I watched, fascinated. The crunch came with tough bidding from both sides. "Six spades," Mother declared, her blue eyes flashing toward T.J.

"Double," said Mrs. Ayers.

"Redouble," replied T.J. He knew Mother remembered and learned from everything—and he didn't doubt his partner's judgment.

"Pass," said Mr. Ayers.

"Seven spades," Mother stated, as if the hand was a lay-down. It was.

I poured another cup of coffee, returned to bed, and dissected the bridge game. My parents' cards had been good but not spectacular yet together they'd bid and made a grand slam. Luck? Not likely. The key was partnership. I phoned Calgary. Dody was at work but could call back at six if I cared to leave a number. I didn't. Flow with the tide: my party was destined to be stag.

Keats arrived first. Since he was several months older, I assumed he knew how to uncork a beer-keg. We watched the fountain cascade down Clancy's sloped doghouse roof and into his bowl. My spaniel lapped voraciously, not knowing the next morning's sunlight would become a painful apparition to cover his paws against.

Robert materialized, turned a screw, and stopped the geyser. "My sister's boyfriend showed me," he muttered.

Richard appeared on the porch. "Got some good ole American corn likker here case you's lacking."

We poured his bourbon into the keg. The doorbell sounded; Alex, as usual, gave a slight bow as he entered.

"I have brought Hungarian pastries, if it is all right."

Richard surveyed the magnanimous offering. "It's *all* right," he salivated.

Ape showed up in clerical garb while Mert wore his commercial team's baseball shirt—a contrast in heavenly versus worldly deliverance.

"If it's Friday," he pointed, "how come you're gonna serve hamburgers?" The accusing finger rose to meet Alfred's head at the hallway door.

"Special dispensation, dear fellow, straight from the Edmonton Archdiocese. In that disgusting situation when Bishop Carroll exempted the St. Mary's football team but forgot St. Joe's, we had no alternative but to stick to our principles and send their tainted meat skyward."

Ape bought it.

"The Archbishop approved?"

"Tit-for-tat," nodded Alfred.

Ape lit the gas-jet under our cast-iron frying pan. Alfred lowered my quizzical eyebrows with a wink. I knew he was lying but it *did* seem a shame to disillusion the pious. Ape looked ecstatic separating ground meat from wax paper—on the forbidden day.

Richard unwrapped a cigar and handed it to me. "You're twenty-one," he grinned, "so let's see if you can act older."

After being assured it would not explode, I lighted the stogie and inhaled. My friends seemed disappointed when I didn't cough, so I took a second confident drag. The room began to spin. Mickey noticed my discomfort and beckoned.

"There's a call for you," he said, guiding my elbow.

I floated toward the hall vestibule, but my brother led me to the upstairs steps. He sounded sympathetic.

"You need to talk to the big white telephone." Mickey preceded me to the bathroom and positioned its small stool beside the toilet bowl. "Sit," he ordered, as he lounged against the sink.

I was annoyed. "Does barfing turn you on?"

"No," he replied, "but since I'm entering the seminary next week this'll be a good chance to bone up on last confessions."

Death *did* seem imminent: the entire bathroom was swaying. I gathered my last resources, and pleaded.

"Little brother, get me out of this and you've got a friend for life."

He rolled his eyes. "I'm thrilled, but your solution's simple."

"What?"

"Snuff the cigar."

I doused the Havana and my nausea cleared. Mickey left.

Keats banged on the door. "Clear out or I'll piss through the keyhole."

I answered with calculated wonderment. "You can squat that high?"

"Jeez," he said, running past. "I was sure my voice changed years ago."

Dave had presaged a ribald evening so I reentered the kitchen with senses alert. Ape absented himself: the conversation was centred on women.

Robert held the floor. "My sister," he hesitated, obviously not wanting to divulge family secrets, "*says* some girls put on new jeans then sit in bathtub water until the pants shrink to fit their butts."

"Is it the same for bras?" Richard wondered.

"No," Robert continued, "but some of them cut the tips off each cup to show a more natural contour under sweaters."

We cited examples. Alex restored reality. "It is sad," he remarked, "that rubbing by wool replaces palmar massage."

Joyous whoops: the Hungarian had mastered our language.

I flipped Ape's hamburgers. Mert's voice rose above the sizzle.

"Speaking of contours, the old neighborhood's changed."

Ape peered through the dining-room doorway. "Bit-by-bit. Jasper Avenue'd be declared a disaster zone if it'd all been destroyed overnight."

Downtown *was* metastasizing outward. Childhood landmarks were disappearing. And the Oliver community, adjacent to the city-core, was not alone: shopping centres had popped up in the suburbs. We and the city were growing together: the changes didn't bother me.

"It's improvement and it's inevitable."

Alex disagreed. "I can't imagine high-rises in medieval Budapest."

"New," Alfred concurred, "isn't necessarily better. Shakespeare at Stratford wouldn't be the same with actors on a screen and the audience wearing 3-D eyeglasses."

Mert brightened. "Think we'll ever get 3-D television?"

"Maybe," said Richard, "they're working on color TV in the States. Late-night movies would be better but I don't think *The $64,000 Question* would be any different."

Long before that show was exposed as a fraud, I had misgivings. A special guest, Randolph Churchill, smiled benignly at the camera and denied knowledge of how the word "boycott" originated. Mickey knew the answer yet Winston's son, having chosen the category "English Language", *apparently* didn't. The moderator was unusually flustered at the denial and cut to a commercial. Later, when court testimony confirmed certain contestants had their questions discussed beforehand, my misgivings turned to admiration: one man's honor could not be bought, even for sixty-four thousand dollars.

Alfred was talking to Mert, so I asked Alex about *his* countryman's performances on TV.

"You watch Ernie Kovacs?"

"I never miss it. There is nothing more hilarious than a weird Hungarian."

We regaled each other with memories. Milk poured *horizontally* from pitcher to glass—Kovacs and the camera were on a mobile tilted set; the comedian furiously working his saw through a branch he was sitting on—and having the tree fall away; his cluster of musical gorillas playing *The Flight Of The Bumblebee* at one note per two seconds—a maddeningly funny scenario.

Smoke wisps, carried inward by breezes through the screen door, saved Ape's dinner from cremation. "Meat's up," I called. Ape disengaged himself from a briefing conversation with Mickey.

Ape took a bite and looked around suspiciously: no one else was indulging. He confronted Alfred. "You sure this is okay?"

"Certainly, old chap, and to prove it I'll join you." He bunned a burger, slathered on ketchup and devoured with satisfaction. "I assure you no mortal sin has been committed."

Ape downed seconds, forgetting Alfred was Anglican. "Strange," he said, surveying the last morsel. "It tastes better on Friday."

The rest of us waited until midnight before indulging.

After the party, I toted my sleeping bag to the back balcony, carefully avoiding folds on the tin surface that could clank and awaken T.J.

Twenty-one at last. The bedroom ceiling had seemed confining and I wanted to survey the sky.

A shooting star skipped like a stone across water. Dozing happily, I heard a guttural moan below.

Clancy's hangover had started.

29 IT'S JUST A MATTER OF TIME

Our genetics lecturer put away her notes long before the allotted hour had elapsed. Elbows resting on a brown manila folder, she stared, then tapped for attention. Unusual. We were silent.

"For us females, tracing origins gets confusing but for you *guys*," she emphasized, "the lineage is straight-line simple. Despite war, disease, famine and natural catastrophes, that male gene you represent has survived: one ancestor in every previous generation sired a son. Go back to perilous North America-bound ocean voyages. Think about the Middle Ages. Consider Roman and Grecian times and wonder, before then, of life in caves or on savannas. Somehow the spark you carry has, against all odds, stayed alive." She gathered her papers and was gone.

I'd never thought of it that way. Grandpa was my *mother's* father and helped guide me through childhood after my father's death. I was curious about the paternal grandfather I hadn't known.

"He died in 1933," Mother said. "I'd never met him but by all accounts he was a character."

Grandfather Edward had decided, in the latter nineteenth century, to establish his dry goods and hardware business in the bustling St. Lawrence town of Cornwall, Ontario. He considered Timothy Eaton demented for attempting the same enterprise upriver in scarcely-civilized York/Toronto. Cornwall was the obvious focal point between Montreal and Ottawa. Grandfather prospered and had been elected Cornwall's mayor. He then bade farewell to his wife Bridget and joined the Klondike gold-rush.

Mother opened her cedar chest. Edward's diary had been preserved. Was I interested in his journey to the Yukon? I apologized after snatching the small book.

It wasn't what I had expected: Edward was more politician than poet, plus he didn't plan ahead too well. His baggage consisted of a large suitcase containing extra business apparel and toiletries, and an empty trunk to bring home the nuggets. Page after page named people he met and topics discussed over and after meals. The train to Vancouver became his Cornwall home, in mobile form, as did the steamship which carried him north to Alaska. Reality evidently set in during his land-trek across the mountainous panhandle. "Fourteen more days of this," he wrote. "Still alive." The memoirs ended abruptly: "Dawson," I deciphered the scribble, "is a hell-hole."

I flipped through blank pages: the return trip was not documented. Bridget, Mother told me, pitied the bedraggled figure on her doorstep and allowed him back in the house. "Their marriage," she added cryptically, "had no further issue."

"Did he get *any* gold?"

"Not then," Mother said, "but later your father, having worked hard here in Edmonton, mailed a ten-dollar gold coin to Cornwall."

I knew what was coming next.

"Learn from your parents," Mother stated. "Disregard us, and you're destined to solving age-old problems your grandparents faced."

"There's no way I'd go camping in the Klondike."

"Perhaps not," Mother replied, "but be aware that the easy path to success is a fantasy."

"You don't have to tell me. Med school's not simple."

Mother frowned. "Just recognize the impulse should it ever arise."

"Why the emphasis?"

"Edward's brother went on the *California* gold rush."

"What happened?"

"Detectives hired by the family located Charles in Los Angeles. Destitute. A hobo. Be warned."

I got the message: my genetics text had one chapter on hereditary traits skipping a generation. "Is that why you sent me to scout camp?"

"Yes." She turned her gas stove's dial and pushed its pilot light button; the lower-left burner ignited. "I wanted you to appreciate civilization."

"And work rather than luck?"

Her eyebrows raised. "You did learn something." She patted the stove. "This appliance was bought, not found."

An alarming connection clicked. I was doomed. "Grandpa Cahill *also* went looking for gold."

"There is a difference. My father shuffled his pan along the North Saskatchewan River as a hobby: Edward's run to the Klondike was an obsession. You've inherited patience and impulsiveness. With one, you might stagnate: with the other you could destruct. Try to find a balance."

I had an unquiet sensation the tides had begun to drift. Mickey's priesthood meant celibacy, so the responsibility for the family genes' continued existence fell on my shoulders or, more closely, hips—a not unpleasant prospect since the university setting seemed programmed toward procreation, our Med Show being the most blatant example.

The revue was raunchy and ticket sales easy: we medical students fostered an impression that sexual encounters elsewhere on campus were at best adolescent fumblings—truth and insight could only be obtained by observing the Education Building auditorium's stage on Thursday and Friday evenings in a mid-February week.

Preparations for the show began with our return from the Christmas break. Each class composed two versions of the same skit. One was for Major Hooper, the university's censor; he tended to ban anything that lacked "artistic merit". Hooper attended dress rehearsals and Thursday's suggestive performance. The original explicit script surfaced Friday, with Hooper safely home in bed.

Our four acts were complemented with a fifth from the nursing students: naughty on Thursday, they embarrassed even us on Friday. The nurses had staked their territory: future hospital relationships would be on a one-to-one equal basis.

My Catholic conscience had kept me off the stage. At seven-thirty I dimmed the theatre and focused a spotlight on our master of ceremonies. Change filters. Emblazon background with red as the curtain opens. Switch angles. Alter colors. Be aware of cues but disregard the ribald proceedings. Dody, of similar mind, was backstage applying makeup to the participants. We met afterward at the Tuck Shop.

My spoon made several extra circles in the coffee. "I've got some good news and some not-so-good news."

"Unburden yourself." Her tone was soothing.

"The word is I'm going to be elected the third-year class president."

"That's great. What's the bad news?"

"One of my duties is to emcee the Med Show."

Dody sipped. "That means you'll be up there telling dirty jokes. We have a problem."

I sensed our relationship was ended. "It's not certain yet."

"You'll win. The problem remains."

I slumped. Dody looked at the ceiling then clinked her cup against mine.

"Got it," she said. "I'll practise."

"What?"

"High-kicks."

"Why?"

"For the chorus line. How else can I join you on stage?"

A kindred soul.

30   LITTLE STAR

I hunched over the medical text on my bedroom desk and tried to study. Impossible. The butterfly had returned: some subconscious conflict required resolution. Lean back in the chair with eyes closed and think. Annoyance—T.J.'s humming signalled his nightly bathroom ablutions had begun: retirement from a post office executive's position didn't alter my stepfather's shave-and-bath ritual. Though he had lost weight and in rare, unguarded moments revealed pain, his general demeanor remained cheerful.

What was troubling my psyche? Exams? No, the second term was going well and learning how to prolong life had become a fascinating project. Romance? No, Dody seemed to understand when workloads curtailed dating. What was it?

The sound of bathtub water splashing muffled as the level rose. T.J. turned off the taps. A brief pause then an alarming vibration shook the upper floor. I sprang across the hall and knocked.

"You okay?" No reply. Try the knob. Bolt-latched inside. "T.J.?" Silence. I stepped back and rammed my shoulder against the door. The lock tore from its frame. I hurtled through. T.J. was unconscious underwater, blood oozing upward from his forehead. A quick flip had him out and prone on the mat. Pump his chest. He coughs. Mother is at the door. "Orange juice and sugar," I ordered automatically. "He's had an insulin reaction." Grab a towel, dry and slip him into the pajama bottoms so he'll regain his senses in dignity. Mother hovers. T.J. awakens.

"What happened?"

"You fainted and almost drowned."

Mother was alarmed. "I'll call an ambulance."

"Never!" T.J. sputtered. "Get more orange juice and you," he pointed, "help me to bed."

I assisted him up and we weaved down the hall.

"*Almost* drowned?" he asked.

"Yep, but I saved you."

"Then you have a lot yet to learn." He settled on the pillows. His gaze fixed suddenly on mine. "Know this: death is sometimes a friend, not an enemy."

The remark hurt. I returned to my room and looked once more at the pathology text's pages. Photographs. Autopsy specimens: at times disease prevailed and there was nothing one could do about it; according to T.J., there were also times nothing *should* be done. I closed the book and went to sleep.

The question did not go away. My impetus for entering medicine derived from the helpless feeling I'd experienced when, at age three and one-half years, I watched my father die at home. Now, my stepfather had rebuked me for saving his life. I needed wider experience and approached Dr. Hanson. Yes, he assured me, a summer job at the Edmonton General Hospital would be arranged.

No application form or references. No pre-employment interview. Just get in the elevator at ten to seven on Monday.

"Sixth floor please."

The operator closed a double-latched cage and swung his lever. "You must be the new lab technician."

"Yeah," I acknowledged with respectful reluctance: this hospital's grapevine was impressive.

We'd been warned. "Hospitals," Dean Scott advised, "are like small towns. News travels with lightning speed among the inhabitants. If a famous personage is brought in by ambulance, the citizens are aware in seconds but," he cautioned, "the outside world encounters difficulty when attempting to obtain information. An invisible boundary separates staff and patients from media and populace. While there are no secrets in a hospital, the institution is a most secretive place."

The elevator shuddered to a halt. "Good luck," its operator said as he unfolded the door. His sincerity echoed a memory—I'd again been welcomed to St. Paul.

Or heaven: the sixth floor was populated by females—a white-garbed angel legion all, it appeared, my age. Back-fastened buttons had separated behind burgeoning bosoms; cotton skirts crept upward, like vines, on nylon legs bent around lab stools; and body contact seemed the rule.

"Excuse me," the brunette apologized as she brushed my arm and thigh, "I've got an elevator to catch." She had six feet of clearance on either side.

A harem, I mused. The eunuch tapped my shoulder. "I'm Edna," she said, tossing her grey pony-tail. "Do you know how to pop a vein?"

"Sure." My bravado surprised me.

"Then here's the tourniquet, tray and morning list. Get these blood samples back here fast."

I'd been assigned boondocks duty: the St. Mary's and St. Joseph's wards were as far as one could travel from E.G.H.'s main buildings without leaving the city block.

Obscure facts, under duress, have a tendency to surface. I recalled that major veins, during gross anatomy dissections, were usually not more than two or three millimeters below skin surface. I angled the needle. Blood flowed. My subject didn't wince—he was in a coma. On to other arms, using previous puncture scabs as guidelines. Quota almost filled, I went down the long corridor to urology's quonset hut. One more sample, but on a fully-alert patient.

The vein bounced right, then left; when finally impaled it yielded nothing. The tattooed man expressed annoyance.

"Look," he said, "these arms are long gone. Kidney stones tend to cause drug addiction. You're better off trying my feet—they've not been used yet."

I slip-knotted the rubber tube around his calf and struck blood on his left foot's dorsum.

"What'll you use when these are gone?"

He replied without hesitation. "My hemorrhoids."

I had, as T.J. inferred, much to learn about the world's traumatic challenges.

Edna gathered my test tubes and divided the specimens. "Hemoglobin on these," she ordered. "White blood cell counts on the rest."

I adjusted my microscope and began tabulations. Awkward. Switch the counter to my left hand. Easier.

"Are you a lefty?" Edna demanded.

"Sometimes," I said. "I bat baseball left-handed and shoot the same in hockey but I take notes with the right."

"Which do you prefer?" She was hostile: in the Fifties, sinister was suspect.

"The hand that seems best for the job," I answered. "Ambidexterity is preferable to left hemiparesis." One-up: Edna retreated in confusion.

I sensed trouble at an adjacent microscope; the prettiest girl in the lab was having difficulty. She grumbled, pushed back her chair and entwined fingers in shoulder-length blonde hair.

"Something wrong?" I asked.

Her lips emitted a litany of oaths: she was a gift-wrapped horsebun, the very antithesis of Mariko.

Mariko was a Japanese exchange student. She would not have passed a beauty pageant's first visual inspection but she had the aura of a survivor. Her quick wit and perceptive mind would still be present long after time had withered competitors' physical attributes. Mariko carried herself with the unusual combination of deferential confidence: upon asking me to demonstrate the technique for smearing a blood spot across a glass slide prior to staining, she added a wrist flick which eliminated all terminal globules. Her result was a text-book perfect specimen.

"Thank you for helping me," she bowed.

Admiration was my only possible response.

Lunch time approached. So did Edna.

"Have a light snack," she advised. "You're the morgue attendant after noon."

"Just for today?" I hoped.

"Every day," she stated. "I won't allow my *girls* near that place."

Discrimination? Possibly, but I could see the reasoning prevalent in this Catholic hospital: Grey Nuns forbade females viewing a nude male body.

Since men were naturally corrupt, my perusal of naked corpses on the autopsy table would not materially alter inevitable damnation. My suspicions were confirmed at noon when Sam Hanson directed me out of the cafeteria's line-up to the doctors' private dining room.

"You can pass," he surveyed my white coat, "as an intern."

I sat. The linen tablecloth had a slight starch odor. Salt and pepper, cream and sugar, and an ashtray flanked the central floral bouquet. No menu. A waitress glided to Dr. Hanson's elbow.

"Yes sir?"

"Today, Marie, I'm in the mood for lamb-chops."

"Certainly." She looked at me. "And you sir?"

Panic—I loathed lamb. "What else is cooking?"

Marie's gaze scalded. "Nothing, now, but I can return later if you wish."

Sam intervened. "Your dinner's cooked-to-order. Name anything."

"Steak please."

Marie nodded. "Porterhouse, T-bone or sirloin?"

"T-bone...and," I caught her inhalation, "medium rare."

"Very good." She returned with bouillabaisse for Sam and French onion soup for me.

Overwhelming. I tapped a silver spoon on the toasted bread's covering of cheese and whispered to Dr. Hanson.

"Is it always like this?"

"Ever since a staff doctor dropped dead in the hallway, our Sisters have been determined to provide us a last hearty meal."

"They figure we're condemned?"

"Don't ask; just enjoy the perks of prejudice."

The meal was free.

We walked down a tunnel to the morgue. A body lay shrouded on the table. Dr. Hanson examined clip-boarded notes.

"Dead on arrival. The police say he tried to set up a homosexual prostitute ring. Evidently, the hetero pimps got to him first. Flip down the sheet."

I thought anatomy lab had steeled me, but now I confronted a horribly-mutilated human whose surface organs had been rearranged. Nausea. I felt a hand on my shoulder.

"You are here," Sam pressed, "and *he* is there. Remember it."

Detachment was the key. Interest replaced repulsion. Which wound had caused death and what weapon was used? Had the killers somewhere left a clue unmasking their anonymity? Would the shredded cloth that Sam found beneath the left index fingernail lead to a conviction?

"*Who*," Dr. Hanson reflected, "was the dilemma in that case. *Why* is what we mostly deal with. Eventually, you begin to hate disease as much as you do criminals."

I concurred. Terminally ill people in the hospital's annexes had a compulsion to talk with me—as if no one else bothered to visit: they gladly yielded a blood sample in exchange for person-to-person contact. Some were frightened, others philosophical. But all were unaware when their decline began to accelerate; I was, and mentioned it to Sam.

"There's a presence of death on the day before they're brought to the morgue."

"Tell me."

"I worked in a produce department and had to check for rotten potatoes by sniffing each bag. The same sickly-sweet smell's in their room when they begin to die."

"Confirm it."

Sam called me into the office several weeks later.

"Dr. Mousseau conveys his thanks. That young fellow you warned me about had silently blown a bowel anastomosis. The Chief suspected something was wrong and didn't need much prodding to do an exploration. He wants to know if you'd consider interning here when you get the parchment."

Dr. Hanson said *when*, not *if*. I would escape Tony's wrath—he had threatened to pulp any class member who flunked. We helped each other sharing notes and insights, and thereby gained time to be squandered, by mutual agreement, on Fridays. Some classmates hadn't attended the inaugural party: they chose to study in isolation and at year's end found themselves tumbled further downward in the posted class rankings. Their response was a lemming-like dash to the library for more, not less, study. Tony had noticed the sporadic hyperactivity and delivered an ultimatum: he would check our eyes for pupil reactions every morning; anyone remotely suspected of having taken speed would be subject to, "...my right hand down your gullet extracting every benzedrine tablet and my left fist pounding your belly to make sure they're all out." Amphetamines were available as "samples" from drug company representatives in each hospital. Tony knew it. We knew Tony. We stayed clean.

I didn't realize how closely-knit our group had become until the morning I was sent to get blood from an emergency patient. I glanced at his name while dashing down the stairwell. It was Alex. My knees felt slippery. *You are here and he is there.* Alex saw me and winced. I was relieved to see him finger the abdomen-prodding staff surgeon as the source of his discomfort. I twisted a tourniquet on his arm. He swung his head.

"Never," Alex confided, "mix paprika and cornflakes."

A voice boomed in the doorway. "Are you the medical student?"

Alex and I both nodded—when Dr. Mousseau spoke, everyone listened. The staff surgeon seemed flustered.

"Simple case of food-poisoning, sir," he said.

The Chief passed an expert hand below Alex's ribcage. Pain. He felt the sweaty brow, and snarled. "Gangrenous gallbladder. Tell the operating room we're on our way."

As Alex was being wheeled out, I heard the Chief confront his underling. "You," Dr. Mousseau's words trembled, "almost let one of *my* boys die." The close-knit family had abruptly expanded.

The next afternoon I went to the surgical ward and checked Alex. Two friends were there.

"How's he doing?"

"Okay," whispered Richard. "He's asleep."

"You sure it's not coma?"

Alfred interjected. "His blissful chuckle after the morphine shot wasn't an agonal response."

"C'mon. I'll buy you guys a coffee."

The cashier waved us past. Richard couldn't believe it.

"Free coffee?"

"They feel sorry for us," I explained.

Mariko was sitting alone, her gaze fixed attentively on a little metal teapot. She'd seen us, but was giving me an excuse to ignore her if I chose.

"Hi, Mariko. Like you to meet a couple more genetic freaks."

Mariko blushed: she'd confided that in her culture anyone *without* an epicanthic eyelid fold was abnormal.

Alfred rolled her name around his tongue. "Must be Japanese." He took her hand. "A pleasure. I'm British."

"I'm American," Richard seemed uncomfortable. "Do you want me to sit somewhere else?"

"Please join us. Why do you say that?"

"After what my people did to yours at Hiroshima and Nagasaki I thought..."

"Do not be troubled. It was good."

Alfred was incredulous. "How can a hundred thousand crispy-fried people be good?"

Mariko's dark eyes flashed. "May I tell you about my country during the war?"

Alfred encouraged her. "As I understand it, Japan was resource-poor and needed colonies much as England did during the Victorian Empire."

"Exactly," Mariko agreed. "Plus it was a religious..." she paused.

"Crusade?" I offered.

"Yes. Emperor Hirohito is regarded as a god. To die defending him was the supreme honor. So we did not fear death."

Richard sat upright. "My uncle was a marine at Guadalcanal. He said the Japs wouldn't surrender."

Mariko disregarded the slur.

"The greatest dishonor," she said, "was to be captured *alive*."

I vouched for her statement: Dody's cousin Herbie had been a Japanese prisoner-of-war for four years, and had not been treated kindly. "Then why," I asked, "did the whole country surrender in 1945?"

Mariko smiled. "We didn't, at least not officially—my country's state of war with Russia still exists in 1959."

"How," Richard asked, "did Hirohito find an honorable way to give up?"

"My father was one of those our Emperor visited after Hiroshima. My father described leaning out of his window to look at the blue-green flash. He told how all his neighbors did the same. They saw the light in the sky..."

"...*and it shone around them*;" Alfred recited with reverence, "*and they were sore afraid.*"

"Yes," Mariko continued, "but it was not until later that the fear became terror."

"Why?"

"My father's head, right arm and chest were blistered at an angle: his legs and left arm were spared. The window-sill was marked on his body. After the Nagasaki bomb our Emperor spoke on radio. We would make peace, he said, with the Americans because they had the weapons to protect us from Russians who were invading our northern islands. We," she bowed to Richard, "chose to fight *with* you, not *against* you."

Richard gloated. "That treaty stopped the Russkies cold."

"And yet," Alfred marvelled, "you're still at war with Russia?"

"Yes," Mariko stated with satisfaction. "Our national honor is preserved."

"Ingenious," I said.

"Diplomacy of the highest degree," Alfred added.

We returned to Alex's room. He was partially awake. Richard recounted Mariko's story. Alex bobbed his head slightly.

"The Hungarian revolution's survivors learned a similar lesson. In wartime, avoid capture and," he mumbled, "in peacetime resist arrest." His eyes closed. Asleep again. We left.

At home, Mother was attempting to break an orange coloring button into white margarine paste; the idea was to simulate butter's natural yellow hue. I took over kneading the plastic bag. Somehow, the ruse didn't seem all that important.

31   THE WAYWARD WIND

There was a future to decide, and my plans included neither building a bomb shelter in the city nor seeking refuge upwind in the wilderness. Atomic war had become a marginal concern, not a continual worry. The optimistic trend was both subtle and contagious: new skyscrapers downtown radiated permanence; suburban houses featured huge plate-glass windows framed by fieldstone; and everywhere dirt or gravelled streets and avenues were being paved.

Pavement created a problem—the city's horses weren't toilet-trained. Excrement that had been pulverized by wheels against stone into golden dust now lay leavening in the sun. Bakeries and dairies were ordered to motorize—invisible pollution was preferable—but the horse routes were already disappearing: bread's cellophane cover and baked-in preservatives delayed blue-green mold longer than did wax-paper; refrigerators *dispensed* ice cubes, so the ice-man was disemployed; and electric fridges in each home made daily milk delivery unnecessary.

As droppings disappeared from the highways, driving became less erratic. Faced with fewer oncoming swerves, Mickey decided it was safe to purchase a Volkswagen—the only affordable new car marketed. Though head-on no match with a V-8, the little car redefined Father Daly's maxim: the shortest distance between two points was a beetle.

Mickey's part-time job earnings hadn't bought the automobile: our maiden aunts' almost simultaneous demise willed a modest inheritance to their nieces and nephews. In a way, Kay and Margaret begat wheels.

The extra car, available for last-minute errands at home, freed T.J.'s Pontiac from its curbside sentry duty. I dated without fear of recall.

An evening spent around the television set was *passé*—and, by implication, nights at the movies were just as bad—the last resorts of those who had nothing to say to each other. Compatibility's true test was a leisurely drive around the city curb-cruising both slums and suburbs. To me, the choice between 96th Street and Wellington Crescent seemed obvious: Dody was not so sure as we parked in front of my rapidly-aging 121 Street abode.

"Remember that drunk we saw on skid-row?"

"Yeah," I replied.

"When you stopped for the red light, I saw him fall down."

"So?"

"Three people from different directions guided him upstairs to his landlady."

"What's the point?"

"On Wellington, a woman walked to her Rolls-Royce and didn't even wave at the man next door trimming his hedge." She hesitated. "Do you know your neighbors?"

I rattled off names and occupations for every house between 102nd and 103rd Avenues.

"Would they help if you collapsed?"

"Sure."

"Are muggings a problem?"

"No."

"Then," she surveyed the boulevard's broad-boughed elms, "you've got the best possible balance right here."

My home, closer to slum than mansion, shone at the moment. We entered.

Mother was in the kitchen, extracting aluminum sock stretchers from woolen footwear. She addressed Dody.

"I hope the new fashion doesn't catch on."

"Calf-length socks?"

"Yes. The ankle's as far as these metal forms reach."

Dress modes *were* changing. Men's coat lapels had plummeted to belt level; the womens' flair skirts became tubular, necessitating an unnatural, knee-locked gait. To compensate, the girls' elongated lower garment sported an extended side zipper. Mother's eyes darted from Dody's hip to me.

"If," she stated, "you plan on playing records in the rec room, leave the door open."

I chucked her cheek. "You like rock and roll?"

"No," she replied with a wink. "Chastity, at this stage, turns me on."

Downstairs, I unveiled my new record-player and the inexpensive portable sound amplifiers on the recreation room's walls. A Fats-Elvis-Buddy sequence sent Dody and me exhausted to the couch. She kept her distance.

"What've you got planned?"

I visually undressed her: she tut-tutted an extended hand.

"Beside that."

"You mean after graduation?"

"What else?" She crossed her legs. Nylon buzzed. The open door kept me stationary.

"It's a problem. I'm too compulsive for general practice: keeping up with treatment advances for *every* illness would mean reading journals twenty-six hours a day."

"So you'll specialize?"

"Got to."

"Internal medicine?"

"No. From what I've seen, the internists are in a holding pattern—their function is to cope, not cure."

"General surgery?"

"The morgue job turned me off guts forever."

"Then what?"

"No idea. Dean Scott told us our future depended on interest and tenacity."

"Where's your strength? The best mark you got was in..."

"...Ralph Shaner's neuroanatomy, so I might end up in research."

"Or neurosurgery."

"Too tough."

I had to resist: neurosurgery in the Fifties was medicine's ultimate disaster zone. There was no reliable method to control brain or spinal cord swelling after tumor removal. If patients lived through their operation, major disabilities were a more frequent sequel than were cures. I had no desire to become a neurosurgeon.

32   BORN TO BE WITH YOU

The call interrupted our canasta game; Mickey answered.

"Are you sure?" He held out the telephone. "Person-to-person from the Vatican. For you."

I took the receiver. Mother left her chair and hovered. T.J. set down his cards. Mickey sat in wonderment. A female operator spoke above the sound of crackling cellophane.

"Is this William, also known as Billy O'Callaghan?"

"Yes."

"The Pontiff will speak to you now."

The Italian accent was exact. "Billy," it pleaded, "how could'a ya do this to me?"

"Do what, Your Holiness?"

"Take one a' my future Mother Generals and getta her engaged."

"We're not engaged yet, only pinned."

Mother was swooning in the doorway. The operator's voice intervened.

"Please deposit another twenty-five cents."

"Where's that damn collection basket. Hokay. Got the quarter." A cash register jingled. "Tella me it ain't so."

"Look Pius," I replied angrily, "think of it this way: we could have twenty kids so you might get ten nuns instead of one."

Mother appeared ready to faint.

"Good idea. Wanna double date at Lakeview this weekend?"

"I'll fix you up with the woman you've been praying for."

T.J. eased Mother to the chesterfield as I hung up the phone.

"*He* called?" she asked. "And you spoke to him like *that*?"

"*He's* back. *That* was Keats."

Third year medicine had started in September, 1959 and now, a month later, mid-term exams were approaching but an evening with Dave and his telephone conspirator was too tempting: we cruised in the Pontiac toward Cooking Lake's dance pavilion.

Dave tapped Dody's shoulder. "You realize," he whispered loudly, "you heartbreaker, what'll happen to the world's male population after you marry this guy?"

"It'll increase," Dody replied confidently.

I heard Keats collapse on the seat. He and Cathy were unnecessarily jocular. "Hold it, you two," I said.

A finger in the rear-view mirror pointed at Dody. "That's *her* job," Keats roared.

I was thankful we'd reached the Lakeview corner. Turn left down a bumpy dirt road. Pass rows of small, closed-for-the-season cottages. Sway into the sand-duned parking lot.

Cold October winds whipped whitecaps along the huge wood pier and sent waves crashing against the pavilion's extended boardwalk. Lights in the circular dancehall glowed through watery mists. Lakeview was a ship on the prairie ready to transport us wherever we desired.

Our ticket was the coat-check stub. No fluorescent wrist dye. No turnstile. An affable bouncer's tattooed forearms guided us on: he seemed flustered as we passed.

"Band cancelled out. A D.J.'s on stage."

Dave whirled in mock-ecstasy. "Omar Blondell?"

"No way," the bouncer sneered. "Lakeview don't do polkas."

We entered during a lull in the music. Pappy and Martha were engaged in verbal fisticuffs over the next selection. Steve. But how? I stood on tip-toes. Ingenious: he was using hand-puppets and a dual microphone; the crowd loved it. Martha was adamant.

"Young people nowadays," she cooed, "need lessons in history. Steven, I demand you play *The Battle of New Orleans*."

Steve's balding head appeared. "You win. I'll have to do it double-length, though."

We knew what he meant. The song was custom-made for bunny-hopping. An enormous line formed. Music. The dancefloor quaked. We applauded the last notes. Pappy surfaced and winked; Martha's head swung round.

"Are you hatching something?"

"No," Pappy cackled. "The kids need geography too. How's about *Kansas City*?"

More applause. Pure rock. We danced. The three hours passed quickly. Dave tugged my sleeve on our way back to the car.

"I watched you two." He patted my shoulder. "You've both made the right choice."

The mid-terms weren't difficult, so I couldn't understand why Tony was frowning as he surveyed the bulletin board.

"Something amiss, most ancient one?"

A beefy finger ran down the list. "Count 'em. Forty-seven originals. They're gonna hit four this year and three the next to get their quota."

I added. He was right. One-third of the initial sixty would fail, as predicted. "What can we do?"

"Go down fighting. Snuff the buggers."

"How?"

"You're the class-president. Figure it out."

Dean Scott was nonplussed when I lay the hit-list on his desk. "This has never happened before. Are they that bad?"

"Worse. The first and second spend all their time discussing rat and rabbit research: we're not studying to be veterinarians. The third is stuck in the 1920's and advocates fresh air for tuberculosis."

"And the fourth?" The dean was intrigued.

"Machine-gunned jargon."

Dr. Scott smiled. "You're asking that lectures be pertinent, up-to-date and comprehensible, I assume."

"Yes sir."

The smile vanished. "I'll get to work on it."

He did; the first three were replaced and the fourth began speaking English. Dean Scott's quiet method was as effective as mouse-guts-on-the-blackboard—and much less messy. The class responded by acing the Christmas exams.

Dody, knowing I'd been preoccupied with my books, offered to help gift-wrap last minute purchases. She swung our garage doors open, as I guided T.J.'s sedan through the narrow gap, then inserted the two-by-four security bar across the doors' metal closure prongs. I struck a match, turned on the corner heater's gas jet and passed flickering flames along the patterned clay elements. We warmed our hands by the fire, not yet willing to enter my eavesdropped home. Under the guise of buying Aunt Lil a brooch, we'd explored Birk's jewellery department. Casual conversation resulted in an unanimous opinion: the fifty-one point engagement ring on display was a craftsman's triumph. In contrast, the one- and two-carat diamonds had been set ostentatiously.

I decided to test the immediate situation.

"Still feel comfortable wearing my med school pin?"

Dody opened her coat and revealed her sweater. "It's here during the day and on my nightie when I'm asleep."

We stamped snow off our footwear on the front porch. Mother didn't mention our bags and parcels—good manners dictated that presents were invisible until wrapped. She had one comment, directed at me.

"You had," her eyes twinkled, "a *bona fide* long distance call."

"From who, I mean, whom?" One had to be careful speaking to a former teacher.

"Red. He and Sue will be back for the holidays." Her lips pursed. "There's only one reason he'd spend good money to announce their arrival."

"What's that?"

"They're expecting a welcoming party."

"We'll handle it." I looked at Dody. "I suspect they've got fifty-one other reasons."

"Agreed," she said.

33   TWILIGHT TIME

We passed Le Marchand Mansion, a Parisian-styled apartment building, and entered Victoria Avenue along the North Saskatchewan River valley's crest. Four o'clock in the afternoon. The sun, having scarcely risen above the distant horizon, began to set, offering in celestial apology, a spectacular ignition throughout clouds overhead. Stark trees cast undulating shadows over snowbanks. Eight hours until midnight. The sky was on fire. I parked: Dody purred in agreement. Surface snow, swept into cake-like frosting by arctic air, reflected colors from the sun and sky. The moment was perfect.

I'd intended to propose marriage nearer midnight but the blue velvet case flipped open in my hand.

We were late for supper. Mother noticed the ring and rose from the table to greet us.

"Congratulations." She pecked my cheek. Dody was embraced. "Welcome to our family."

Florence and T.J. departed early for the Ayers' party down the block. I washed dishes while Dody wiped and stacked. The doorbell sounded, one long and one short: our 115th Street gang's secret signal.

"Red's arrived."

"Dody pocketed her diamond. "Let's not upstage them. Make it *their* night." She had class.

I dried my hands. "Put your ring on and don't worry. You've never met Red. Chances are Sue's got an even bigger rock." She had.

Our excited exchanges were interrupted by crowds at the door. The downstairs filled. Records played. Tantalizing odors wafted from the kitchen; I investigated.

George, a classmate of French-Canadian descent, was cooking pancakes.

"Traditional," he remarked, "on New Year's Eve."

One batch burned. Red and I sought fresh air on the back porch's laundry platform. We sat, neither knowing what to say, and watched large, fluffy snowflakes descend around us. A raucous cheer from inside broke our concentration. Red turned to me.

"Sort of strange, isn't it?"

"What?"

"You and I've been thousands of miles apart yet we've both ended up engaged at the same time. What's with us, that we all think alike?"

I recalled Father Fee's comment in the same location.

"You think," I asked, "there's something wrong with us guys?"

Red raised his eyebrows. "Not wrong. Different from the past but alike among ourselves." He tilted his head as familiar sounds issued from the doorway. "Let's go in and welcome the Sixties."

We stood up in response to our music: the Archbishop had been amazingly perceptive.